NORFOLK CHURCHES

Their foundations, architecture and furnishings

by

H. O. MANSFIELD

Foreword by Lady Harrod

TERENCE DALTON LIMITED
LAVENHAM . SUFFOLK
1976

Published by
TERENCE DALTON LIMITED
ISBN 0 900963 57 3

Text set in 11/12 pt. Baskerville

Printed in Great Britain at
THE LAVENHAM PRESS LIMITED
LAVENHAM   SUFFOLK

Contents

Index of Illustrations

A serious house on serious earth it is
In whose blent air all our compulsions meet,
Are recognised, and robed as destinies.
And that much never can be obsolete,
Since someone will for ever be surprising
A hunger in himself to be more serious,
And, gravitating with it to this ground
Which, he once heard, was proper to grow wise in,
If only that so many dead lie round.

Philip Larkin
Church Going

No one can understand history without continually
relating the long periods which are constantly
mentioned, to the experience of our own short
lives. Five years is a lot. Twenty years is the horizon
of most people. Fifty years is antiquity.

Sir Winston Churchill
The Birth of Britain

Foreword

THIS is an amazingly comprehensive book, touching on every aspect of Norfolk churches, from iconography to barrel organs and from the Saxons to the pre-Raphaelites. The author is particularly fond of the Saxons and has very personal theories about their influence on Norfolk church building. His ideas will probably provoke controversy — no harm in this — and books about churches usually do. But no one will want to deny the vast amount of work Mr Mansfield has done; and he has done it with great enthusiasm and affection, which is passed on to the reader. I am proud to write this foreword and very glad to think that this book will be circulating in Norfolk for many years, helping people to find and enjoy the infinite variety of wonderful things there are in our Norfolk churches, which are the finest attraction our county possesses and worthy of our greatest appreciation and care.

	WILHELMINE HARROD
The Old Rectory	Chairman of the Committee
Holt	for Country Churches
Norfolk	The Norfolk Society

———————

In memory of my father

Charles Mansfield

whose love for Norfolk and its churches

was the real genesis of this book

Preface

"NORFOLK is one of the great architectural treasures of Europe because of its mediaeval country churches." So wrote Sir John Betjeman, the Poet Laureate, in a Foreword to *Norfolk County Churches and Their Future*, published by the Norfolk Society in 1972. He went on to say that, in their profusion lay their greatness, and added that every Norfolk church left standing, however dim, neglected and forgotten it looked, was loved by someone or it would have disappeared long ago.

The substance of this work is very much an attempt to justify both assertions of Sir John's and to show how much of Norfolk's past has continued, despite vicissitudes, to remain enshrined in her churches. Modern archaeological research yearly uncovers more and more of our remote past. The church is so often the living monument to the centuries between, revealing sometimes more than it hides but often offering enigmas hard to solve.

Many churches, solid looking though they appear to be, have been headaches throughout the centuries since their foundation for even in mediaeval times jerry building was not unknown. In some the soling and heeling that has taken place from the thirteenth century onwards and particularly during the nineteenth has left a myriad question marks. Norfolk flint rubble walls are easy targets for the restorer: so long as you keep the rubble watertight you may make what alterations you wish, a fact of which the Victorians certainly took advantage.

Today many of our Norfolk churches are faced with more potent a foe than restoration. Redundancy is now a word of omen for those who love our heritage of church architecture. It poses a universal threat more dire than any since the Reformation. At its worst the threat of redundancy creates in the mind a state of indecision and lack of confidence which in turn brings about considerable local indifference. Since 1968 when the important piece of ecclesiastical legislation known as the Pastoral Measure was promulgated, redundancy has hung like a thunderhead over many a Norfolk church. A Pastoral Committee was charged with the responsibility of recommending which churches were not to be retained as places of worship; in turn a Redundant Churches Advisory Board then was to decide which of the redundant churches were of such historical and architectural importance that they should be preserved. In cases where structural changes were proposed in favour of some alternate use, whether those changes were acceptable. Other redundant churches deemed worthy of preservation would be vested in a Redundant Church Fund which would thereafter be responsible for repair and future maintenance of the buildings and contents. By late 1972 only thirteen churches were 'under care'. The ultimate total is expected to be between three and four hundred.

These facts are the mere skeleton of the scheme yet it nonetheless presents a desolate picture. It would be heartbreaking too were it not for the considerable body of voluntary aid that has, in consequence, sprung into being. For example, a branch of the Norfolk Society known as the Committee for Norfolk Churches, under the Chairmanship of Lady Harrod, has been active in the preservation of a number of churches whose fate hung in the balance. In some cases the Committee's inspiration has succeeded in stirring local consciences and awakening again in villagers a love, lapsed but still latent, of the church in their midst. In such human action lies a glimmer of hope for the future, at least until the Church Militant once more sharpens and polishes its sword.

I have tried to keep the use of architectural terms to a minimum throughout this work. Those used are embodied in a Glossary of Terms. By my general use of the word Saxo-Norman I have risked the derision of the pundits, but, seeing more of humanity than of art in most mediaeval churches I have persisted in employing the term widely to include work occurring between A.D. 1050 and 1200. My reason should be obvious if you bear in mind that so plastic a thing as language to a great extent repelled the impact of the Norman invaders. Thomas the Rhymer who died in 1299 wrote in quaint but pure English. Robert de Brunne, born 1303, wrote ". . . for the love of simple men that strange words cannot ken." Langland was most vigorously and truly English, using an alliterative style that was purely Saxon. Chaucer, 1328-1400, wrote an English as easily understandable to his Saxon forefathers as it is to us today. With such evidence of Saxon lingual tenacity, why must the purists so casually dismiss evidence of a similar continuity in Saxon art and architecture which they superimposed upon the basic Norman Romanesque like delicate gilt tooling upon a calf bound volume?

It should be borne in mind that the Conqueror may have brought from Normandy his master mason or, for that matter, an army of masons yet they must have been fully engaged in the vast building schemes occasioned by military needs and by cathedral and monastic demands. To argue that every little parish proceeded to employ Norman masons is therefore ridiculous. Primarily it was the Saxon who was the artist. That his art was influenced by continental culture is fundamentally true from the seventh century onwards but his work was often incomparably finer than anything continental artists of the time were producing. It is for this reason I have ignored the slim differences between Saxon and Norman workmanship in our Norfolk churches.

It is my earnest wish that my readers may be helped to enjoy each his own pilgrimage around the county. Unfortunately, present conditions inhibit the freedom we once enjoyed. Widespread vandalism and theft is such that police advise that village churches shall be kept locked when not in use for services. This is why I have refrained from mentioning church plate or any article of such intrinsic value as might catch the eye of thieves or of an organiser of thieves. Perhaps another day may dawn when we shall achieve once more that placid haven of security where such measures may be necessary no longer. Meanwhile, in some cases, police restrictions have been overcome by parishioners themselves who have voluntarily provided warden service in their beloved church during certain hours of the day.

A word regarding illustrations. I have avoided providing a series of exteriors and interiors nor have I provided pictures of outstanding or well-known features. I look upon pictures and their captions as guide-lines to help the reader identify common artistic, architectural, ritualistic and iconographic details. With these he should be able to go out and read a church's history and architecture for himself. The majority are my own and Mr James Oates' work and for a few I am indebted to Eastern Counties Newspapers, the Colman and Rye Library and the British Museum.

Finally I wish to acknowledge my indebtedness to the many who have given generously of their time and help in the compiling of this work. My thanks go first to the Norwich City Library, to Mr Philip Hepworth, to Mr Frank Sayer and his assistants in the Colman and Rye section for their unfailing assistance. I should like to thank the many rectors and vicars I have met who have been happy to discuss their individual churches with me: and the Very Reverend Gilbert Thurlow, Dean of Gloucester, for his emphatic encouragement. In particular I would mention with gratitude Mr A. B. Whittingham, M.A., F.S.A., A.R.I.B.A., Consultant Archaeologist to the Dean and Chapels of Norwich Cathedral. He has read, criticised and commented upon my typescript and I have been only too happy to avail myself of his wide experience and to make use of his valuable suggestions. Finally I must mention Mr Ralph Bootman of Stoke Holy Cross, Norwich who has kindly made available for me a list of little histories of many Norfolk church organs.

I have completed an accompanying Gazetteer of Norfolk Churches together with additional illustrations which I hope will be published later.

The Dim Beginnings

ATTEMPTS to fathom the birth of Christian faith in Norfolk have to be made under such misty conditions that they usually end up much as though one stirred up with a stick the muddy depths of a pond in the hope of getting clear water. It may be said that at least until the end of the sixth century whatever occurred in the eastern sector of the country was an echo of what was happening at large in the south of Britain. While it can be argued that East Anglia stood at the fore-front of Christianity in the seventh century, evidence leans towards the possibility of its having been as well the last stronghold of paganism. So much for clarity of outline. Material evidence is so scanty while myth is as tantalisingly misleading.

Absence of stone throughout the region is a great handicap to research. Buildings of wood, wattle-and-daub and clay lump, unless given loving care, quickly disintegrate or can be easily destroyed, wood leaving no more significant trace than a stain in the ground. However skilful the Saxon became in later centuries — and there is considerable evidence that he did erect astoundingly impressive structures in wood — fire was the inevitable enemy.

The Mediaeval builder must bear blame for a lot of our ignorance concerning earlier church construction. His aim was primarily to build nobly for the glory of God and his only indestructables were the site hallowed by usage and the dead who lay in serried ranks in their last sleep within that hallowed site. Where money came easily — as it did in East Anglia in the fifteenth century — the master crafts-man was encouraged to clear the site. Who knows how thorough was the clear-ance he made? Who can tell what secrets he buried? It is left to whoever may in the future remove what is now standing to witness the unveiling of the past. Only then would it be possible to formulate tenable theories on the extent of the Christian ethos in Norfolk. We can but speculate on what might lie hidden.

That Christianity existed in Britain during the Roman occupation is today an undisputed fact. How widespread it was, how far it successfully competed with the indigenous beliefs of the British and the Roman pantheism is not clear. It is impossible to state with certainty that the remains of, or the foundations of any building associated with the period are those of a Christian church. Even Silchester is open to doubt. Though Christianity was a living faith from the early days of the Empire, celebration of its liturgy, which consisted of readings from the Apostolic Gospel writers and the writings of the Fathers of the Church and the taking of the Sacramental Meal all must have occurred under conditions similar to those in Jerusalem at the time of the Apostles, that is, in the room of a house. What tangible evidence we possess in East Anglia consists of the six Mildenhall Treasure spoons inscribed with the sacred symbol of Christ, the Chi-Rho monogram set between the Greek letters alpha and omega, the Icklingham lead font bearing on its front panel the Chi-Rho monogram, a pewter dish from a Fenland farmstead and a gold ring from Brancaster. These merely indicate a family character of local Romano-British Christianity.

The Mildenhall Treasure, comprising a quantity of silver ware, was turned up by deep ploughing in 1942 close to the remains of a fourth century Roman building. Chief glory of the collection was a massive silver dish almost twenty four inches in diameter and weighing over eighteen pounds. In relief upon its surface is a scene depicting Bacchus the wine god triumphing over a drunken Hercules. God and hero are naked among dancing satyrs and the god Pan. In addition to this remarkable piece are dishes, bowls, plates and goblets but of importance to our purpose are the six silver christening spoons, three of which are marked in the bowls with the Chi-Rho monogram set between the letters alpha and omega.

All the pieces, pagan and Christian alike, were buried together. They represent wealth, culture and perhaps a large degree of religious tolerance. The richness of the hoard suggests that the owner possessed power and influence. The burying implies the sudden appearance of danger allied to the hope that, with the return of a settled peace, life could be continued as before.

It was again a Roman building at Icklingham in Suffolk that yielded in 1939 the circular lead vessel assumed to be a font. It is made of three pieces of lead sheeting. One circular piece forms the base and two rectangular pieces jointed form the sides. It is about two feet eight inches in diameter and thirteen inches deep. Around the rim is a moulding of cable pattern while a series of vertical ribs with zig-zag decoration divide the sides into ten panels. These ribs appear to simulate linen straps and the vessel might be assumed, for no clear reason, to imitate a leather or cloth water holder supported within a rope and webbing frame. One panel bears the Chi-Rho monogram, M with A and O, the corresponding panel at the back the monogram alone. It could have been in its day a costly article; obviously it was owned by a Christian.

These were the property of wealthy folk but further evidence points to a lower level of society being Christian. From a farm at Welney in the Fens comes a pewter dish with Chi-Rho symbols while at Brancaster, the Roman fort of Branodunum on the north Norfolk coast there turns up a signet ring. The seal bears two heads and the words VIVAS IN DEO — "May you live in God" — a form of salutation only to be found among members of a Christian community.

From this archaeological evidence I consider there emerges the picture of a faith spread broadly throughout the social spectrum, among the rich and the merchant classes, among rural communities and in military camps while the most humble members of Romano-British society scratched the sacred monogram upon rough pieces of pottery. I think it fair to assume that we have not seen the last of finds of this nature in Norfolk. That they will strengthen assumptions already formed, that they will help eliminate a few more of the dark shadows in the picture is true, but can they add much more factual knowledge regarding Christianity in Britain during that remote period of our history?

Extending our search for the moment beyond the bounds of East Anglia, there is evidence of the finding of the Chi-Rho monogram on the decorated plaster of the walls of villas and hidden amid the intricate patterning of tessellated pavements. Additional to this there exists a singular word square that only in recent years has been proved a secret Christian symbol. It takes the following form:—

R O T A S
O P E R A
T E N E T
A R E P O
S A T O R

The translation of the square as it stands is innocuous and purposely misleading. *Rotas opera tenet arepo sator* can mean "The sower Arepo holds the wheels carefully". If we accept the assumption that AREPO is formed from a Celtic word for a wheeled plough an alternative translation produces "The sower guides the wheels for the plough carefully".

The subtlety of the word square is that it can be read similarly in four ways, down from the left, up from the right, across left from the top and right from the bottom. Casual observers would dub the thing a word game of the character of a multiple palindrome. In 1925 it was found that the letters could be rearranged in the form of a cross to make the word PATERNOSTER twice, using the N centrally for each arm. This left two A's and two O's, the Alpha and Omega of the Greek alphabet which refer to the Book of Revelation 1 v. 8 where occurs the passage "I am Alpha and Omega, the beginning and the ending, saith the Lord."

```
                          A
                          .
                          P
                          A
                          T
                          E
                          R
        A . P A T E R N O S T E R . O
                          O
                          S
                          T
                          E
                          R
                          .
                          O
```

The presence of this word square was first noted on the walls of a house in Pompeii, the city destroyed by the great eruption of Vesuvius in A.D. 79. It is possible to have dated it from the period of Nero's persecution of the Christians in the late sixties of that century. Important to us, however, is the fact that this same word square appears on the plaster of a room in a Roman villa in Cirencester and could have been inscribed there at any time in the third and fourth centuries but dating probably from the time of the Diocletian persecutions. What both discovery and persecution postulates is the presence, not of a handful of the faithful but of important Christian communities for surely persecution only occurs when numbers of the persecuted are large enough to threaten and frighten the persecutors. Gildas, writing in the sixth century mentions that in Britain many churches were destroyed at the time of the persecutions but that these were later rebuilt and many new ones erected. Bede tells us that not until Constantine had restored recognition of the Christian faith was the church at Verulamium built.

Another piece of evidence exists pointing to the importance of the Christian communities in Roman Britain. Three bishops from the island attended the Council of Arles in Gaul in A.D. 314, the Bishop of Londinium, the Bishop of Eboracum (York) and Adelphus who could have been either Bishop of Lincoln or of Camulodunum (Colchester). The last was of such importance that he had a priest and a deacon to attend him.

This summoning of bishops suggests to us the existence of an organisation that could only have been engendered in the soil of a widespread and long standing faith. We know that they attended with the power to discuss and mould trends of thought for they joined in condemnation of the growth of Arianism and they helped fix the date of the Easter celebration.

Again, Tertullian in A.D. 208 and Origen in A.D. 230 wrote that the Christian religion had an appreciable number of converts in the remote province of the North west — and Britain was that extreme North west province. It seems that the third century of the Christian era, in contrast with all that had gone before, was indeed a Golden Age for Britain in both a material and a spiritual sense for undoubtedly the advent of the fourth century witnessed the beginning of a decline. The power of Rome received blows, internal and external; security was being lost; the day of the isolated villa was gone and men sought the safety of towns; there were whispers of fear all around and the shadow of the barbarian began to hover over the land.

After the final departure of the Roman power at the beginning of the fifth century popular history paints the picture of a Dark Age when hordes of Saxons beat back the helpless British to the Welsh mountain fastnesses and obliterated or let fall into ruin the cultural centres left by the Romans. Present day archaeology is revealing sufficient evidence to make this picture far too naive to be accepted. The inroads of the barbarians were without doubt severe. The Picts and Scots pressed continually on Hadrian's Wall. The Saxons, a virile, lusty, land-hungry barbarian race, pressed even harder on the coast from Northumberland to Dover. People came to live under the same sort of menace from the sea as today modern nations do from the air. Probably tides of refugees ebbed and flowed, fleeing from one savage onslaught after another, halting again some distance away in comparative safety, returning at the first signs of relaxation of pressure to the land they had tilled and the life they had known. The sorry picture has been painted so often in our enlightened twentieth century, in Europe in the wake of two world wars, in Korea, in Vietnam, in Bangladesh. Invasion never exterminates a people. Millions may be killed but always some remain or return to keep alight the flickering flame of their culture.

It is reasonably certain that, after the final exodus of Rome, cities and townships remained to some extent intact and unchanged for nearly a century. In the year when Germanus visited the country, the British under his leadership — for he had in early life been a Roman military leader — defeated a combined force of Picts and Saxons in what has come to be known as the Hallelujah Battle. Strong evidence exists for supposing that London held out for long against the tide of Saxon invasion for continental writers speak of its value as a centre of trade. Though the British kings Lud and Bellinus, commemorated in the names Ludgate and Billingsgate, may be more legendary than real, there must be some strong reason for the survival of their names. There is significance in the penny struck by King Alfred in London mint that bears London's name in interlocked letters of strangely Roman design. What were the special rights — described as being immemorial — which William the Conqueror ratified in his Charter? And why are English kings and queens always met by London's chief magistrate at the city's gates? Is the custom a relic of ancient treaties under which its independent inhabitants maintained relationship with Saxon kings? However significant the questions may be we have no factual answer to them.

What can be accepted without doubt is that Britain in the fifth century grew into a loose confederacy of communities in which the communal element became weaker as the monarchical element grew stronger. Amid this subtle revolution the only imperial sized organisation left from the fall of Rome was the church and that being so it is most unlikely that its hold upon Britain would be willingly relinquished. Slight evidence in Norfolk goes to show that memory of the church did not go completely under the tide of paganism. The name of Eccles occurring near Attleborough and near Hickling could point to the presence of some form of ecclesiastical building remaining from Roman times. The term 'castra' occurs twice, at Caister near Yarmouth and at Caistor St Edmund near Norwich. In Roman times these towns performed different roles, the one primarily a port that could have been engaged in continental as well as coastal trade; the other a cantonal military town built specifically to maintain control over the great grain growing district peopled by the Iceni. Geological changes could have brought about the eventual run-down of Caister by Yarmouth but we know that Caistor near Norwich remained both as cantonal capital and market town. When, after A.D. 360 occupation was on a much diminished scale, the rural economy continued to flourish around it. The point about both is that their identity remained sufficiently long after the Saxon invasion for their names to have become embedded as it were in the invaders' own language. A moribund ruin would not have made so strong an impression on a race superstitious yet ruthless and indifferent to death.

There can be another theory to account for the perpetuation of these names. It could be that, when at a later date, Saxon communities grew up alongside or within a short distance of these deserted towns, there remained some form of Christian building which, after a general conversion and baptism, could be restored to use. At Caister by Yarmouth a church, Holy Trinity — the dedication has a Saxo-British ring about it — stands immediately above a portion of the Roman town. At Caistor by Norwich the little church of St Edmund — this dedication has a tenth century significance — stands at one corner of the fortified town, within the very walls themselves.

Towards the end of the fourth century the Romans brought in *foederati,* that is mercenaries, from Schleswig-Holstein to strengthen the east coast defences against raids by the Picts and Saxons. Though it is impossible to be dogmatic, it is fairly certain that these Teutons could have eventually settled down and married British women, some of whom might have been Christian. Their settlements are known to have often been sited by Roman lines of communication. Here small pieces of evidence slot into place. Roman siting posts were held to be 'sancta' and as such were in consequence left alone. Now if we take a straight line between

Caistor St Edmund and Reedham we find almost equally spaced and in line, churches of Framingham Earl, Ashby and Carleton St Peter. The dedications, Andrew, Mary and John the Baptist, are all typical of early Saxon foundations. Bearing in mind that just over the border in Suffolk are two churches, Ilketshall St Lawrence and St George, Stow Langtoft, both built on Roman siting posts, it is reasonable to surmise that the foundations of all four churches mentioned could rest on similar sites.

It cannot be argued with certainty that any form of British-cum-Saxon church was built during the fifth century. But it can be maintained that superstition and memory kept alive the sanctity of the siting post around which a Saxon community had developed and that when in the seventh and eighth centuries Christianity demanded a church, the site of it would be accepted without argument.

By the time the Saxons were being converted during the early part of the seventh century many towns and villas would still be standing, ruinous, yes, but undisturbed. Less superstitious than their pagan grandparents, these new Christians must have looked upon such crumbled monuments with awe rather than with fear. Bede tells us that they restored and reoccupied former Romano-British churches that had long been neglected.

It is, alas, impossible to bridge the gap of a century that lies between those who fought against extinction almost into the sixth century and the first evidence we have of the Christian faith being brought to the Saxons at the beginning of the seventh. All we can go upon is the fact that, in some Saxon cemeteries, evidence turns up of later burials being orientated and of this custom becoming fixed. Other than this, nothing linguistically or politically illumines in the feeblest way the dark of that hundred years. One might describe it as the abyss between Rome, pagan and imperial and Rome, papal and missionary.

Although this gap appears brutally apparent and although no documentary evidence exists to alter in any way accepted historical interpretation of the period it would yet require much to convince me that Romano-British Christianity completely faded out. I feel certain that some debased form of the faith lingered on, making easy those early contacts by Celtic and Gallic missionaries and their establishing of crude monastic clusters. The later Augustine mission was going to need these earlier established centres of faith more than just Raedwald's half-hearted conversion to maintain a toe-hold between A.D. 600 and A.D. 630. The organisation of the Gallic Church under the leadership of St Felix lasted until the Mercians drove it out in A.D. 650. The defeat was no real triumph for paganism. The quick re-establishment of Christianity proved this and shows that St Felix himself had laboured in no vacuum or total wasteland. His efforts would have lasted less than a year amid a people completely antagonistic and unwilling to accept a new religion fundamentally opposed to their ancient forms of worship.

At this point it is worth while speculating for a moment on how a church came to be established during those dark distant days, for, if their dedications mean anything at all, they probably began life in the seventh century. In the very dawn of Christianity people probably gathered around a small portable altar like that of St Cuthbert in Durham Cathedral or like the Crusaders' wooden chest-altar in Newport church on the Essex-Hertfordshire border. It would be set up in the open at the foot of a rude cross. Exposure to the vagaries of British weather was not the only hazard. Such conditions of worship were too much akin to those which the evangelists sought to eliminate. So the next development was the building of a small chapel to protect the altar. Moreover, in the sixth century Gallo-Roman bishops had already protested against the British practice of carrying around portable altars. (E. L. Cutts, *Parish Priests and their People,* 1898). It has been suggested that from this fact arose the mediaeval custom of the rector being responsible for the chancel and the parisoners for the nave. Whatever the origin this custom had a marked effect upon the growth of the English parish church as can be seen by comparing the E.E. chancel of Blakeney St Nicholas with the majestic nave built later by its wealthy fifteenth century parishioners.

Snettisham St Mary: one of Norfolk's more noble churches. Rare features are the spire supported with flying buttresses and the West Galilee porch.

CHAPTER ONE

The Saxon Diocese of East Anglia

IT MUST have been a quirk of fate that, although the sixth century could appear disastrous, it was not to prove calamitous. Christianity and culture fell back, the former only to recede, the latter almost to die. Ruin and death followed as a wave of barbarians had swept the country. Yet by the fifth century, though they still came as before, their purpose was now not to plunder, burn and steal. They had become land hungry men leaving their barren acres for the fat pastures of Britain. The Saxon was a valley dweller, his ideal a water meadow for hay, lower slopes for the plough and the hills for pasture. East Anglia, the granary of the Romans, was his for the taking. While work of clearance was in progress the Saxon kept his British serfs busy on their hill farms. Then when the valleys were ready for sowing all came and clustered down by the stream. So it has come about that occasionally names of hill, wood and stream show some British links, but village names are invariably Saxon.

With the fall of Rome the only visible organisation left seemed to be the church. For those suffering the turmoil of Saxon inroads, Christianity may have appeared a better cross to cling to than the moribund polytheism of the Romans.

Twilight had indeed fallen upon the island the Romans called Albion. It had enjoyed four hundred years of order, prosperity and culture. It had seen well-planned cities with temples, markets and academies. They had encouraged crafts-men and merchants, professors of literature and medicine and rhetoric. Now all had vanished. With the coming of the evil days the British church went underground or fled to the west. More than two centuries were to elapse between the departure of imperial and pagan Rome and the arrival of papal and missionary Rome. St David accomplished the general conversion of what is now Wales. St Patrick, after years of slavery came under the influence of St Germanus, was converted and baptised and in A.D. 432 returned to Ireland and brought it into elusive contact with the church of Western Europe. From Ireland his followers carried the gospel across the narrow seas to what is now Scotland. There Columba, born fifty years after Patrick, established a monastery on Iona whence his disciples were to spread the faith over Strathclyde and eventually into the Saxon kingdom of Northumbria. It was a Christianity monastic in form having little or no Roman contact nor was it until later to be associated with the universal organisation of the Papacy.

We like to think in these days that nearly all change is far less perceptible to those who live through it than it appears to be in hindsight. To some extent this could have been true regarding the state of the Christian church during that dark fifth century. It seems that towards its end missionaries from the north, Aidan, Cuthbert, Cedd and Chad must have succeeded in finding contacts in East Anglia. Bede tells us that when the Saxons had been converted they restored or re-occupied former Romano-British temples. Alas, so ferocious were raids of the Norsemen in the ninth century, the possibility of any building sacred to the faith remaining from that remote period is infinitesimal. As the raids of earlier Saxons had obliterated Roman culture so the Norsemen even more thoroughly destroyed material memorials of work of such pioneers as Aidan, Augustine, Paulinus and Theodore of Tarsus. Small wonder that the words of terror, "From the fury of the Norsemen, good Lord, deliver us" were put into the Litany. It is to Theodore we owe the organisation of our episcopal system, an organisation of fourteen bishops. Probably even parochial organisation followed at a more leisurely pace. Yet Norfolk stands unique among counties in the possession of ruins of the Saxon minster of North Elmham and of other churches exhibiting signs of Saxon origin that will be dealt with in due course.

The evidence of history, however tenuous, of archaeology and of hearsay or legend all point to one thing. Christianity did not die under the hammer blows of the Saxons. Towards the end of the sixth century Pope Gregory sent Augustine to begin a mission in Kent and with orders to make a priest named Mellitus the metropolitan bishop of London. Why, if imperial London was in ruins should Gregory have given such an order? A man would hardly be eligible for such distinction unless there existed an organisation large enough to warrant the elevation of its leader. Augustine disobeyed the order making Mellitus only a suffragan bishop, but the ceremony was conducted on the site of St Pauls, then reputed to be the site of a temple to the goddess Diana. We know too that Augustine summoned a conference of Christian bishops and they met somewhere in the Severn valley. Had Augustine come to a completely pagan island where would he have found the bishops? The picture becomes one, not of extermination of the British by the Saxons but of fusion with them and of a slow, almost imperceptible absorption of relics of Romano-British culture and faith that only needed the spark of missionary endeavour to fan into flame once more.

Pope Gregory's instructions to Augustine were clear and illuminating. "Do not pull down the fanes. Destroy the idols, purify temples with holy water; set relics there and let them become temples of the true God. So the people will have no need to change their place of concourse and where of old they worshipped demons let them continue to resort on the day of the saint to whom the church is dedicated and slay their beasts no longer as a sacrifice but for a social meal in honour of Him whom they now worship."

A vague indication of this antiquity of some churches in East Anglia can be gained from dedications used in conjunction with a study of village names. Place names are an essential part of our language. In many cases they are the oldest spellings of oft repeated words we have in our language. Naturally some are more successful representations of the spoken word than others and here it is possible to reconstruct the original word or at least get close to it.

Mention has already been made of the British word egles (itself a corruption of the Greco/Latin Ekklesia, a church). This word has come down to us twice in Norfolk in its Saxon form of Eccles. Now no clear indication exists that the Britons, despite their obvious survival, exercised any appreciable influence on the eventual Saxon language. Four hundred years of Roman overlordship had already gone some way to Latinise the aboriginal tongue. The new and far more virile conquerors were unlikely to accept other than stray words into their own patois.

Consequently most place names are Saxon in origin, connected loosely with the basic name of the tribe or the thegn who had made the area his homestead. Where in the word the old Saxon genitive 'inga' occurs (as in Hindringham, Sheringham and in some 60 other Norfolk village names) experts think that these represent the settlements of early waves of immigrants. Now it is known that when Christianity first spread among the Saxons the earliest dedications used were those of St Mary, All Saints and the more popular apostles. Of 58 villages in the county containing 'ing' in their names it is therefore significant that 21 churches have dedications to St Andrew and 28 to St Mary. Bear in mind that the earliest conversions must have been made by Celtic monks from the north and it becomes clear why St Andrew should be dominant. It is reasonable to assume that not until the tenth century, during the time of the great Saxon church building expansion did Saxon dedications such as Etheldreda, Walstan, Winnold and Wandregesilius, Botolph, Chad and Edmund become adopted.

Of the slow conversion of the Saxons the picture that takes shadowy shape throughout the sixth century is one that underlines the tribute we should pay to the boundless faith and indomitable perseverance and fearlessness of that small handful of Christian missionaries. From the wild Saxon viewpoint their spiritual power must have seemed born of the most potent magic. By comparison their work was as great as was that of Victorian missionaries in darkest Africa. We are left breathless at the power of those few gentle, unarmed men whose faith made them persuasive enough to outface and overcome the superstition, the mental terror, the ruthlessness and the sheer physical brutality of the Saxon thegn.

To understand the mass conversions often mentioned by chroniclers it is necessary to look at the Saxon mentality that could make them possible. The thegn was all-powerful. Men would fight to the death for him, never accepting possibility of defeat. They modelled every act of their turbulent lives upon him.

He was pagan, so were all his followers. But were he moved to adopt Christianity and be baptised then one and all lined up at the river. A completely illiterate community, seeing their equally illiterate but lusty leader bending the ear to a shaven priest who could read and interpret what he read to the level of under-standing of his listener, would be shaken by such awesome magic. In mass they witnessed the baptism — such ceremonies were conducted in the open air for the very reason that they felt the potency of these magicians was strengthened within a building — and were only too eager to share in its magical benefits. Mark you, should the initial meeting have gone the opposite way they would just as jubilantly have helped in splitting the priests to the chine with their axes.

In this super loyalty to the chief we can witness the beginnings of the political ties that have always bound together Church and Crown. Once Saxon East Anglia had come to accept the faith it is possible to see links being forged with the royal house of the Wuffings. Its inception takes us back into the sixth century when the chief Wehha first amalgamated the individual tribal families of the area into a loose confederation. Wehha's descendant, Wuffa, died around A.D. 580 and his successor, Tyttla, about A.D. 600. Raedwald, the first shadowy figure to take historical shape, was baptised a nominal Christian early in the seventh century. Bede tells us he " . . . had been admitted to the sacrament of the Christian faith in Kent, but in vain, for on his return home he was seduced by his wife and certain perverse teachers and turned back from the sincerity of the faith . . . In the same temple he had an altar to sacrifice to Christ and another to offer victims to devils: which temple Aldwulf, king of that same province, who lived in our time, testifies had stood until his time and that he had seen it as a boy."

This assessment of Bede's is undoubtedly a biased opinion of Raedwald's character. Whatever his faults he was a ruler of ability, by far the most powerful and successful king produced by the Wuffings dynasty. As Bretwalda, or High King, the only East Anglian to achieve this position, he succeeded in welding under his rule the other adjacent Saxon kingdoms, thus for the first time creating a unity of the Anglian tribes that did not break up when later it came under the vassalage of Penda of Mercia. That Raedwald attempted to make the best of both pagan and Christian worlds is a measure of his ability as a ruler in such a time of flux.

Aldwulf was the grandson of Raedwald's brother, Eni. He died in A.D. 713 so quite possibly was born about A.D. 650. It would seem from his testimony that Raedwald's temple could have been a Romano-British building adapted to pagan worship but with a subsidiary Christian altar. Here is revealed the possibility of a survival of debased Christian practices though Bede, who was about forty years old when Aldwulf died, has nothing additional to say. However, Aldwulf's account of this survival is contemporary and as such may be accepted.

It is difficult to sort out the successors of Raedwald and Eni. Many got killed either in battle or by the assassin's axe. Most were Christians of sorts, largely through the good offices of Edwin, King of Northumbria. At that time a Celtic Christian, he was the dominating influence in the country. In A.D. 633 he and his elder son Osfrith were killed in battle fighting against Penda, King of Mercia. Penda was probably the greatest of the seventh century kings and appeared to be an inveterate opponent of Christianity. His powerful influence caused the temporary disappearance underground of Celtic Christianity both in Northumbria and in East Anglia and the retreat to Canterbury of the Augustine mission. Three years were to elapse before Sigeberht — either cousin or brother to the last East Anglian king is not clear — returned from banishment among the Franks to assume the crown.

By all accounts Sigeberht was a most pious Christian and a learned man. He was responsible for asking Archbishop Honorious of the Gallic church to send St Felix to East Anglia and he established the saint at Dummoc which was for a period to become the centre of the diocese. Some doubt exists whether Dummoc was Dunwich or Felixstowe but as Bede calls it a *civitas* it must have been a former Roman town. Rigold suggests it was Walton Castle, a Saxon shore fort near Felixstowe which was destroyed by the sea in the eighteenth century.

At Dummoc Felix baptised and taught for seventeen years. Tradition says that he was responsible for other churches and monasteries. SS Peter and Paul at Shernborne is reputed to be on the site of the second church built by him and he is also said to have founded a monastery at Reedham. These we can accept more easily if it is true that he first set foot on East Anglian soil at Babingley.

About the same time an Irish monk named Fursa left his country to preach and evangelise among the Saxons. He reached East Anglia and Sigeberht gave permission for him to build a monastery within the walls of the old Roman fort at Burgh Castle, beside the River Waveney. Recent excavation at Burgh Castle has revealed a Christian cemetery and some plaster and post holes of a wooden building. It was characteristic of Celtic monasteries to be built within fortified areas. Probably North Elmham had been a fortified earthwork. If description of Fursa can be accepted, he was, in effect a sombre missionary. He maintained that he had descended into Hell and for ever after to have borne on his face the marks of the infernal flames. In all probability he had suffered partial martyrdom by fire at the hands of pagans whom he was trying to convert, had escaped with his life and lived to profit by his disfigurement. Throughout his time in East Anglia he represented the Celtic church influence as manifested through Aidan but for all that he was held in great veneration by the Gallic Bishop of Dummoc and the Papal Archbishop of Canterbury. On his return to Gaul he was succeeded by his half brother Fiollan, another Celtic monk from Iona and two Irish priests, Gobban and Decuil.

It must be assumed that Sigeberht favoured the Celtic church organisation which centred around monasticism for in A.D. 636 he founded a monastery at

Burgh Castle, Roman fort of Gariannonum, in which King Sigeberht allowed St Fursa to build a monastery.

what is now Bury St Edmunds. There he retired in order to pursue a religious life, having made over the kingdom to Ecgric, his cousin, who had previously been governing a province of the kingdom. However, by A.D. 640 he was called from his monastic seclusion. Penda, King of the Mercians had attacked East Anglia again and the tribal leaders begged Sigeberht to take his place at the head of troops defending the country. When he declined they took him forcibly from the cloister. It is said that he went into battle carrying no more than a wand in his hand lest any man's blood be upon his head. Both he and Ecgric were killed in the battle and the cloud of paganism thickened over the land for a spell.

The Crown now reverted to the sons of Eni, Raedwald's brother. Bede tells us that Anna was a good and active Christian who founded a monastery at Blythburgh in Suffolk and added stately buildings to Fursa's monastery at Burgh Castle. During Anna's overlordship as vassal of Penda, and probably until A.D. 655 when the Mercian power was destroyed, Christianity apparently existed under sufferance. Yet it is hard to correlate what political evidence we possess of the period with the existence of monasteries such as Ely, Blythburgh, Burgh Castle and Bury and the fact that widows and unmarried daughters of the ruling classes generally took the veil and often became abbesses. It poses the question whether Penda's lifelong war was levelled more against the growing temporal power of the Church militant rather than against those who piously but quietly practised the faith. Bede tells us that he did not oppose the teaching of Christianity but he despised those Christians who lacked "works of faith."

In fact there is no hint in Bede or any other historian that the East Anglian ever lapsed into paganism in time of trouble. The outstanding figures in recorded history of this period of flux are not the kings but the men who cemented the bonds of faith under their protection, Felix, Fursa and another not previously mentioned, Botolph of Icanho, whose fame as an organiser of monastic life spread throughout England and who became one of the favoured saints of later Saxon dedications. Bede, in his Historica Ecclesiastica, tells us that his Abbot, Ceolfrith, visited St Botolph in East Anglia before A.D. 716 while an aged brother in the monastery had seen St Fursa and heard him tell of his visions.

East Dereham: the Holy Well just west of the church. Said to have been the site of St Withburga's tomb.

Anna's eldest daughter, Sexburgh, married the King of Kent, was later an abbess of Ely in succession to her sister Aethelthrith, while another sister became Abbess of Brie in France. Anna's youngest daughter, Withburga, founded a convent at East Dereham. In A.D. 654, there she was buried and miracles were performed at her shrine. Pilgrims came from afar for whom rest houses were erected that could have laid the foundation of the town. In the tenth century an abbot of Ely sent his monks to steal St Withburga's body and lay it beside those of her sisters. Legend tells that a spring of water issued from her empty tomb and to this day her well may be seen in a vaulted undercroft just below the great west door of Dereham church, its stonework fern fringed and spangled where tiny flowers shine amid the lichen and moss. Both Saxon nunnery and the original church were destroyed by the Danes.

Little more can be learned from the Historia Ecclesiastica but from another of Bede's works known as the "Eight Questions" we find mention of a volume containing many pictures representing the Labours of St Paul, brought from Rome by Cuthwine who was Bishop of East Anglia somewhere between A.D. 716 and A.D. 731. Here is evidence that one East Anglian bishop visited Rome. This book later returned to the continent probably during the East Anglian mission there in the eighth century.

After Bede we have no more narrative sources of information regarding East Anglia. Only episcopal lists have survived because they were inserted in a Mercian compilation drawn up around A.D. 790. One eighth century work, the Vita Sancti Guthlaci, originally written by St Felix, has survived. From it we get some insight into what books were then available for Felix refers to other English scholars, proving that he was not the only man of letters in East Anglia. King Aelfwald commissioned the book. He had, together with the *abbatia* (higher clergy) written to St Boniface between A.D. 742 and A.D. 749. His letter stated that prayers for the saint's safety in Germany had been said for him in seven monasteries, one of which was Icanho. In A.D. 803 the Elmham contingent to the synod of Clofeshoh consisted of the bishop, four priests and two deacons whereas the Bishop of Dummoc took with him two abbots and four priests. This suggests that the two most important monasteries were in the diocese of Dummoc. Clofeshoh and other synods imply that East Anglia was undoubtedly influential outside its borders in the late seventh century.

It is at this point in the evolvement of our East Anglian diocese that cautious mention must be made of the great ship burial at Sutton Hoo near Woodbridge because it brings to light material evidence of the peculiar alliance between Christianity and paganism still existing in the minds of men throughout that dark period and, for that matter, far beyond. Undoubtedly the sandy plateau above the River Deben's estuary was the necropolis of the Wuffing kings. The numerous barrows may have bridged the whole period of the dynasty. The paradox of the ship burial, revealed in 1939, is that such a burial should have occurred at all in an area where, by contemporary accounts, Christianity was becoming established among the Saxons. Here was a burial in heathen tradition and of surpassing richness. But whose cenotaph was it? By all the superficial evidence of a ship burial it was that of a pagan king. Yet amid the collection of grave goods, all intended to accompany that anonymous monarch to his Valhalla there are bowls incised with equal armed crosses, christening spoons inscribed with the names Paulos and Saulos (in Greek characters) placed at what would be thought of as the dead man's shoulder, had a body been there. Equal armed crosses form a basic design of the scabbard bosses. Such objects as these could never have been the burial accompaniments of a king before Raedwald.

Everything about the burial points to Raedwald, apart from the Christian objects. Both standard and whetstone sceptre could well be symbolic of his high office as Bretwalda. But where was the body? If the minute quantity of bone ash found on or near the Anastasius silver dish points to the remote possibility of a cremation then we are faced with the added paradox of a unique mixture of two opposed concepts, a cremation incompatible with Christian custom and a burial without the burning of the accompanying grave goods contrary to pagan practice.

The 37 gold coins together with the three blanks found in the purse have in recent years given a pointer to the possibility of Raedwald being the king for whom the ship burial was intended. If the burial was c. 625 − 30, then these coins − a miserable collection by comparison with the character of the rest of the grave goods − were of roughly the same date. Dr Philip Grierson has put forward the theory that the purpose of the coins − the number having been deliberately made up to 40 with the addition of the three blanks − was symbolic wages for the 40 oarsmen concerned in taking the ship to its last resting place; like gifts to Cheiron, ferryman of the River Styx. A last word comes from the Swedish archaeologist, Sune Lindqvist. He points out that though the ship burial in some ways reflects Swedish pagan practice, he saw in much a typically Christian arrangement of grave goods only conceivable during a period of transition.

So we are left with this question. Could the burial be the irrational behaviour of a people under stress? Did the shock of some disaster cause a reversion to an ancient type of funerary ritual? Perhaps these questions may possibly be answered by a glance at that greatest of all Saxon poems, *Beowulf.*

The Beowulf story came to East Anglia as a fully developed piece of Scandinavian work recalling the ancestors of the reigning monarchy. The *mise en scene* is fundamentally Scandinavian but the conduct of the story, the courtly diction and the general tone of the poem has been anglicised. The character of Beowulf himself paradoxically teeters between pagan and Christian concepts. Out of the hero-figure beloved of Teutonic peoples emerges the man willing to sacrifice his life, not for personal glory but to preserve others from the powers of evil. The metre of the poem, its notes of reflection, the quiet dignity and leisurely pageantry, all are remote from Norse poetry. They suggest the recording of a tradition long known but brought up to date, like a translation of Chaucer into modern English. Was it the Wuffings who introduced the story relating to their ancestors in Geatland and now naturalised in East Anglia? Evidence from Sutton Hoo suggests that during the lifetime of those who remembered the building and furnishing of the barrow a poet composed *Beowulf* for a member of the royal line to glorify his family and to offset the already flowing tide of Christianity.

On this note we can leave the subject of pagan influence in East Anglia. It was about this time that there took place an important conference which finally settled the lines organised Christianity was to take. In A.D. 664, at the Synod of Whitby, the hinging issue was whether British Christianity should conform to the general plan of Christendom or whether it should be dominated by the monastic orders which had founded the Celtic Churches of the North. The outcome was that the Church of Northumbria should in future be an integral part of the Church of Rome. So a decisive step had been taken in the spiritual sphere and the temporal powers of papal Rome were established in Britain.

In certain respects the Synod of Whitby represented an overt criticism from Rome of the part played by both Augustine and Paulinus. From the beginning they had centred their efforts upon guiding and governing British Christianity from Kent. In A.D. 688 two new emissaries were chosen to carry the torch into the northern mists, Theodore of Tarsus and Adrian of Carthage. What a picture these appointments reveal of the universal character of seventh century church government. Could we imagine today a Syrian Archbishop of Canterbury and an African Bishop of London — or for that matter at any time since A.D. 1066? Only three bishops greeted them on their arrival in Britain but by the time of his death in A.D. 690, Theodore had raised the number of British bishops from seven to fourteen and by his organising skill had given the church a new cohesion. By contrast the political scene was still to be torn apart by intricate rivalry between various Saxon kings and split by tribal, territorial, dynastic and personal feuds, with seven kingdoms of varying strength all professing Christ and striving by fraud and force to gain mastery over each other.

One surprising feature of the time is the number of amazing journeys performed either on foot or on mule or horse. When we realise that a major part of the country was heath, forest or marsh, that the few existing townships were clearings in this green jungle, one can only assume that, despite all superstitious prejudice, the Saxons kept serviceable in one way or another the great Roman roads even when, as we know, they closed certain sections with ramparts across them. Priests, monks, bishops and saints thought nothing of journeying between

Canterbury and York or Hereford. How could the armies of Mercia, Northumbria, Wessex and East Anglia have been moved had they not made use of the road system? Theodore of Tarsus could never have organised his episcopal system without means of communication. Even the Venerable Bede, in his monastic fastness of Jarrow could not have compiled his monumental history but for the scores of scribes who at one time or another visited him from the far corners of the country. In that period of political tyranny and violence it is almost a paradox that the more peaceful sections of the population could traverse the country in comparative safety. It proves that close by those roads that threaded the country there existed refuges where travellers could find hospitality, for the cross country journeys of those days must have taken weeks to accomplish. We can only assume that they were monastic foundations of sorts, clusters of wooden buildings around a tall church of wood, whose broached steeple rose above the surrounding woodland. It all emphasises that age-old quality of the human spirit that ensured the continuance of faith despite the violence of political unrest.

Within twenty-five years of the coming of Felix the ungainly diocese administered from Dummoc was divided. The action looks like having been one of the early readjustments made by Theodore in pursuit of better organisation and a consolidation of ecclesiastical power in an area where Celtic and Gallic liturgy still held sway. It is unlikely that poor communications were the reason. East Anglia from Roman times had been the heaviest populated of any part of Britain other than Kent, and roads, except where they had been ramparted must, as I have said, been kept open. The new diocesan centre was at North Elmham and I see in this a possible effort to counteract the Celtic minster still existing at South Elmham in Suffolk and the provision of a separate diocese for the North Folk.

As the ruins appear today, neither could have been built earlier than c.1040. What there was before no one can tell with certainty. Both had a Bishop's gallery — or pew — built into the tower and approached by a stairway, an innovation from Carolingian France.

Howbeit, the See of Dummoc continued to function from A.D. 637 till A.D. 870 and North Elmham maintained a succession of bishops until A.D. 824 when the Danes sacked and burnt the minster, a proof that the building could have been a wooden structure. Dr Wade Martin states, (*Norfolk Archaeology,* Vol. 35 Pt. 3) that the cessation of the bishopric occurred soon after the last attestation of Bishop Humberht in A.D. 839. Some buildings were burned down and the hilltop abandoned. This was once thought to be the time when the Bishop's Throne, now in Norwich Cathedral, was damaged by fire but modern opinion leans towards its being the fire damage of 1463.

Within a hundred years the new bishopric was functioning, united for a short time again with Dummoc. The cathedral was probably rebuilt — still in wood — on the site of the existing stone building. At the same time a Bishop's Palace, grouped around a large courtyard, was erected. Thereafter succession continued uninterrupted until eleven years after the Conquest, when Bishop Herfast, Chaplain to William the Conqueror, transferred the See to Thetford. His reason was two-fold, economic and political. Thetford was at the time the most flourishing Saxon town in East Anglia, having 947 burgesses and 13 churches, surpassing in size and distinction Norwich. The latter was still licking its wounds and struggling to regain its commercial prosperity after the sacking and burning by Swein Forkbeard in A.D. 1004.* Of greater import for Herfast was the growing prestige of the great monastery of St Edmundsbury. King Canute had a deep affection for St Edmundsbury. In A.D. 1020 he granted by statute four pence a year to the monastery on each carucate of land in East Anglia. In 1081 William in Council decided that Bury was free from episcopal control because Bishop Ailwin had granted that freedom. Nonetheless the regal grant ended in 1096 when Herbert de Losinga got it transferred to Norwich to help pay for his new cathedral. Abbot Baldwin visited the Pope to reinforce his exemption from episcopal jurisdiction but he never got back his four pence per carucate. He probably relinquished it in order to settle the more parochial dispute that might have rankled for years.

This conflict between bishop and abbot reveals that the church in mediaeval times was to a large degree bedevilled by the struggle for power between the regular and secular priesthoods, that is, between the mitred abbot and the crosiered bishop. It was a conflict of loyalties. Monastic loyalty was primarily slanted towards enhancement of the Order; secular loyalty leaned towards Canterbury and the Monarch. Under a strong king both regulars and seculars vied to obtain the king's ear. As only the priesthood was literate in every sense of the word it mattered not so far as the king was concerned who were his advisers. Herfast's move had been as much an effort to check the spreading power of Bury as to bring the cathedral of the diocese from an area of comparatively shrinking importance to one of commercial and economic life. As we have seen, the move lasted only nineteen years. Herfast and his successor, William de Beaufeu, failed signally to check the prestige of St Edmundsbury or to prevent its ownership of what amounted eventually to 40 manors in Norfolk. Herbert de Losinga, though he committed simony by paying to William II a high price for the See, acted in a far more politic way by transferring the See to Norwich. Moreover, according to Domesday Book William I had already granted land for the foundation. Then too, the large number of Royal servants he established in Norwich proves the monastery to have been accepted as a Royal foundation.

The story is an interesting one in that it illustrates the divergent tensions of power that in those days entangled men in authority. De Losinga was in all

*Thetford had also been sacked twice, in 1004 and in 1012 but had probably escaped burning.

probability an East Anglian — despite his Norman name — who was destined from youth for the church. He was educated in France at Fécamp, a Benedictine house but recently established. In A.D. 1088 he came to England and was made Abbot of Ramsey in Hampshire. That he committed simony three years later by making the highest offer for the See of Norwich is more fact than legend. That his sin troubled his mind to the extent that he had to obtain absolution from the Pope is also fact. He set out with that intention and on his way through France he met his king. Rufus forbade him continue his journey but he persisted and then settled the problem his own way. At the time there were two Popes, one the redoubtable Gregory VII, enemy of corruption within the church, the other a cypher set up by Henry IV, the Holy Roman Emperor. De Losinga wisely decided in favour of Gregory's rival who absolved him — an action Gregory would have found impossible — reinvested him and laid upon him, as penance, the task of building a cathedral at Norwich.

The reasons for the choice of Norwich were twofold. Thetford as a dominant commercial centre was in decline, Norwich had shaken off the disaster of 1004 and was literally a boom town with 1320 burgesses to its credit and a king's representative dwelling in all the panoply of military might right in the town's centre. From an ecclesiastical viewpoint this was important. With the Holy Roman Emperor and the Pope at loggerheads it was necessary that the diocese be linked in harmony with the monarchy. But the other factor was, if anything, of even weightier consideration. De Losinga was a Benedictine; he had been first Prior, then Abbot of Benedictine houses. The Benedictines were monastically all powerful and their declared policy was to move from the seclusion of the countryside and establish themselves in towns. As backing for this, Archbishop Lanfranc was himself a monk and favoured the idea that cathedrals should be served by monks. More important still was the fact that, as head of a monastic cathedral he combined regular and secular roles, being both Abbot and Bishop.

There was no confusion of loyalties in de Losinga's make-up. The combination of See and monastery was an essential part of his long term plan. The formal transference of the See took place in 1094 and two years later the Bishop laid the foundation stone of his new church. So rapidly was the east end and the crossing erected that consecration took place on 24th September, 1101, the church being dedicated to the Holy and Undivided Trinity. That the proper rendering of worship might be maintained the Bishop attached to the cathedral a body of sixty monks, providing for them claustral buildings on the south side in conformity with the basic Benedictine plan. To secure for the monks all the benefits he had designed for them the Charter of Foundation was provisionally signed and later confirmed in full Parliament, subscribed to by 33 witnesses.

The great Founder Bishop died in 1119 having been in office twenty-nine years. So remarkable a man had he been that the anniversary of his death was kept, marked by particularly solemn services. He had been a man of untiring industry, an organiser of great ability, deeply religious, but one who did not continually talk about holy things — in fact he was a Christian with a character eminently East Anglian.

Thirty-three years before Bishop Herbert's death the Domesday Book had been compiled and accepted by the king at Winchester. Complaint is often made that only a small number of churches is mentioned in the compilation. Understandable this, for Domesday Book is an inventory of property, an assessment of the plunder acquired by the Conquest, a golden book evaluating the pirate's hoard. Where churches owned land and paid gold for it they were mentioned; where they appeared to the assessors more of a liability than an asset they were ignored. Some church land was described as *Libera Terra*. For example this applied to the 'free land' at Mulbarton although it had been held by Roger Bigod's predecessor and Roger was himself holding it in 1086. In actual fact this *Libera Terra* was probably a piece of Saxon gerrymandering for we find a sokeman, having *given* a carucate (100 acres) of free land to the Abbey of St Benet at Holme, was still holding it of the abbey. Of the 116 Norfolk churches for which value is given in Domesday Book, 44 are valued at a penny an acre and several at twopence. An additional 144 are mentioned as of no value. In a number of the 'breves' we are told, "All the churches are valued with the manors whose headquarters they serve."

Throughout the mediaeval period, and for three hundred years after, the diocese of Norwich included both Suffolk and Norfolk. At the present time there has been created a new diocese for Suffolk in the See of St Edmundsbury and Ipswich. Norwich still retains those Suffolk churches in the Isle of Lothingland in the vicinity of and including Lowestoft. On the other hand a large piece of Norfolk west of Swaffham and south of Lynn and embracing the whole of the Lynn marshland has been transferred to the Diocese of Ely.

CHAPTER TWO

The pre-Gothic Church and Byzantine Influence

BEFORE we can comprehend fully all that the mediaeval church means to us today we have to gain some understanding regarding church building before the Norman Conquest. Unless we can be sure that a church was founded after the twelfth century it will undoubtedly have beneath its flooring remains of the foundations of a Saxon church or possibly of a building even earlier. Moreover, whatever happened architecturally before 1066 had later influence upon design and certainly, in many cases, upon area dimensions.

I am constantly going to use the term Saxo-Norman although I realise that, by so doing, I am blurring the change in styles from the Saxon mannerisms to the Norman, styles that have clear distinctions. This has not been done to confuse the issue. I accept that there were those changes in styles but I do not accept that an army of masons descended upon England and the poor Saxon ceased working. Norman masons were employed upon the great monastic and cathedral projects but the artificers, the sculptors, the workers and carvers were Saxon. When it came to the little parish church they were solely responsible for the work. What is more, the influence that we today call Norman had begun to infiltrate this land many years before the final Norman Conquest. So, under this umbrella term, Saxo-Norman, I cover the years from 1050 (?) to 1200.

The flow of influence from the continent was even then nothing new. Throughout the two great blossomings of Anglo-Saxon art the standards achieved, though always bearing the stamp of Mediterranean art, were incomparably finer than anything contemporary continental artists were achieving.

A common feature of Saxo-Norman church building before and after the Conquest was the apse. Students of architecture all accept it as evidence of antiquity. At first glance it appears a cumbrous, inharmonious excrescence, an incomplete building of which half is missing. Externally it looks a graceless bulge, internally it creates the impression of being a frame to house some object of veneration. The old gods of Babylon were always framed in an apse though their statues were small in comparison with those of the Greek world. The Romans, feeling their way towards the development of their arcuated designs discovered the tunnel vault which in turn led to the dome. By erecting a semi-circular recess and covering it with a half dome they rediscovered the apse.

Both Greek and Roman used the apse as the common feature of a spacious building, religious or secular. The Roman Hall of Justice was provided with an apse around which sat the magistrates. All large buildings of the period possessing the exceptional merit of spaciousness and elaboration were given the name of basilicas. The name comes from the Greek work "Basilion" meaning a king. Thus they were simply halls fit for a monarch. To this day St Peter's at Rome is known as a basilica.

Jewish synagogues were buildings contemporary with Greek temples and Roman basilicas. They were rectangular buildings designed to accommodate numbers of worshippers under cover.

The roof was carried on classical columns surrounded on all sides with lean-to roofs while on one side only was an apse shut off with doors or a curtain to house their most sacred possessions, the Rolls of the Law. In front of the apse rose a *bema,* or raised reading desk approached by steps from the front of the apse. This was to become the basic design of the early Christian church.

From earliest days Christian worship was conducted under cover in contrast with pagan practice before altars in the open. The basic form of worship apart from readings from the Apostolic writings and from the Fathers of the Church, was the Sacramental Meal. Not until Christianity under Constantine the Great became the state religion of Rome did the architects of the Imperial City realise the problems set them by congregational worship on an imperial scale. They had suddenly to design and build covered accommodation to meet the new demand. Consequently the vast buildings they first erected were on the lines of the Jewish synagogue, rectangular, columned, with aisles, a large *bema* and an apse, orientated to the east. At the entrance to the apse was placed the *mensa,* the sacred table for the Sacramental Meal. Around the apse sat officiating priests while from the *bema* the choir intoned music based on the Ambrosian modes and the scriptures were read or intoned.

Until Constantine moved his capital to the shores of the Bosphorus, these were the great churches of Rome, a city that was later to become a ghost town, not to recover its grandeur for a thousand years.

Roman temples of this country were small and square, surrounded with a verandah in imitation of the classical peristyle. Foundations of one were uncovered at Caistor St Edmund in 1930. St Augustine could have seen many of these still standing — and in some cases being used as Christian churches. He ordered the building of a number of churches along the South-east coast which were all rectangular rooms with apses orientated to the east. The remaining three sides were surrounded with a pillared inward looking verandah or porticus. At the time they were built they must have looked lofty and impressive.

During the following half century other similar churches must have been erected in the wake of Augustine's monks. Most were of wood. Some, like Bradwell in Essex and Bradford on Avon, could have used worked freestone from nearby Roman buildings. Most, however, were built of rough fieldstone for as yet no freestone for mason work existed and brick making had almost vanished with the Legions.

Although there is great diversity of opinion on the dating of St Mary, Cockley Cley I feel that there we possess what could be an example of the church of this period. By a supreme whim of chance it seems to have been saved as evidence of this remote time. At the Reformation it was converted to secular use, becoming a house for the parish priest. A Tudor chimney was built on the south wall and a large kitchen chimney went up through the nave arch. To accommodate a second storey the roof was lifted three feet while the south door was blocked and its recess used as an oven. The building was occupied as a cottage until 1948 since when loving restoration has been carried out in the course of which many interesting architectural points have been laid bare for discussion. Original windows were found lacking all evidence of stone quoins but edged with flint and small broken stone at the meeting of splays and wall. A variable splay of the west and north windows was unique. Clearly it was intended to throw as much light as possible into the dark interior of the apse. Acting on the assumption that the apse might have been a twelfth century addition the join-work between nave and apse was carefully studied. It was found that both stone and mortar used were identical and of the earlier period. The proportions of St Mary are 1 x 1.50 which agree with the Augustinian churches of St Pancras, Canterbury (597) and St Andrews, Rochester (604). The apse is clearly of Augustine type.

Not only does the structure fit in well with the period but all points to its having been built between A.D. 600 and A.D. 630. This inevitably leads to its association with Raedwald, that extraordinary East Anglian king who stands colossus-like between Saxon paganism and Christianity. His kingdom, extending west into what is now Bedfordshire and northwards to the borders of Northumbria, was concentrated in three main areas one of which was that of Cockley Cley-Narford of west Norfolk, probably one of his more prosperous regions. After his marriage to a Kentish princess and his conversion, he returned, accompanied by priests, to this part of Norfolk and there gave permission for the church to be erected on the site of a previous temple or perhaps a Celtic Christian church, for beneath the foundations of this present building there are reported to be foundations still older.

Sir Peter Roberts of Cockley Cley Hall maintains that *no* round apses were built in East Anglia between A.D. 630 and A.D. 1000. He argues that the Augustine influence over East Anglia lasted only from A.D. 600 to A.D. 630. Moreover

Cockley Cley St Mary. Primitive chancel arch with imposts. Looking west.

Romano-British and Celtic churches were rectangular. There followed the brief period when the Gallic Church under King Sigeberht occupied East Anglia and Felix became Bishop of Dummoc, but this was suppressed by the Mercians about A.D. 650. After this any church building, until the arrival of the Danes, was in wood.

To make this later church building clear we must turn back the centuries for a moment. In discovering and establishing their barrel vault the Romans revealed the possibility of a dome. Byzantine architecture perfected the dome and in so doing evolved a centralised building, bringing worshippers into a compact area. The Roman basilica had forced an extension away from the altar; the centralised, cruciform church brought worshippers together. But more emphatically the dome taught another dominant lesson, that of building vertically rather than horizontally. It established the Christian church as a towering structure piling itself upwards towards a central feature.

The cruciform idea spread westward as Europe, under Charlemagne's influence, attained a measure of peace. Away from Jerusalem all churches had to be aligned along an eastern axis so, in consequence, the Byzantine church had to have an eastern apse.

How did the idea of loftiness engendered by the dome reach East Anglia and what results did it have? Byzantine influence had bypassed Rome as the Holy Roman Empire shifted influence away from Italy towards the Rhineland. Charlemagne's Chapel at Aachen is pure Byzantine. The Western world, while accepting the Pope's spiritual leadership became in material respects a counterpart of the greater empire and followed as best it could the architectural fashions set by that great civilisation. But without stone, the dome suffered a sea change, transmuted into a towering structure in wood.

Turn to the Lindisfarne Gospels and the Book of Kells — now considered to have originated in Northumbria and dating from the end of the eighth century, together with Echternach and Durham Gospels — and see exhibited the vibrant orientalism reached by Anglo-Saxon art. It was objects more than artists that carried eastern ideas westward so that Roman saints and eastern vine scrolls became inextricably mixed with Celtic bosses and interlaced and strapped motifs. In such settings the saints depicted, with eyes unseeing and drapery conventional, might be copies of the fifth century mosaic figures in Ravenna.

In the ninth and tenth centuries, Anglo-Saxon England, artistic, industrious, wealthy, had absorbed these numerous artistic influences flowing in from the Byzantine east via Northern Italy and Provence, that most advanced province of Gaul, and from the Ottonian part of the Holy Roman Empire. The simple Celtic churches of the past were superseded by towering structures in wood that must have dominated the countryside. None remains in Norfolk. Only Essex possesses a few minor relics, notably at Stock, West Hanningfield and Blackmore. These have no complete chancels as little of the timber structure has been preserved, and today act as bell towers at the west end of stone naves. One may be allowed the remote surmise that wooden structures within towers as, for example at Aylsham and Cawston, where they serve as supports for ringing chambers, might have been part of earlier turreted structures, or if not, have been copied from remains of them.

With Saxon posted construction the great timber tower could reasonably have been surrounded with aisles in imitation of a large Byzantine church in exactly the same way as can be seen in some twelfth and thirteenth century barns. In these the crutches were carried down leaving on either side aisle-like space for the stacking of corn. In the Saxon church the outer walling would have been of timber or stone, or compromising, there could have been a low stone wall on which rested sleeper beams. Timber framing would rise from this as in many an East Anglian barn and farmhouse today.

The end of the eighth century had witnessed a great resurgence of church building throughout the western world. It found its counterpart in England. In Norfolk the age-old conflict between Celtic and Romish liturgies was long past. Churches such as Cockley Cley had disappeared, to be replaced by towering structures. The pure Byzantine cruciform, turreted church was however, less strong an influence on architectural design. It took only tenuous hold in Norfolk and must have been impressive. It was usual for Saxon transept arches to be narrow. Norman transept arches by contrast were as wide as the tower itself. St Mary, Flitcham is a remaining example of the latter and St Lawrence, Castle Rising later still. At Flitcham the massive central tower reveals shallow blank arcading and stripwork typical of Saxon thought. The north and south transepts, on the basis of vestigial Y tracery is dismissed as thirteenth century whereas evidence from the foundations should have been investigated. There remain however the two distinct types of which there can be no question, the axial type with a tower between nave and chancel but no transept and the cross plan with transepts.

A feature of a number of Norfolk churches, pointing to obvious Saxon origin, is close grouping. Where this happens the dedications are Saxon in almost every case. The Reepham cluster contains St Mary, Whitwell St Michael and the remains of Hackford church, ruined since 1543. At South Walsham, only 30 yards from each other are St Mary and St Lawrence while at Antingham are St Mary and ruined St Margaret in the same church yard. Beechamwell has St Mary, St Martin (now ruined) and St Botolph (almost completely disappeared). In north west Norfolk the Wiggenhalls have St Mary the Virgin, St Mary Magdalen, St Peter and, most significant of all, St Germanus. Gillingham, Mundham, Tivet-shall, Warham and Weeting all have, or have had two churches and all the

Part of the Shotesham cluster in winter. Shotesham St Mary and, near by, the ruin of St Martin. *By courtesy of Eastern Counties Newspapers.*

dedications point to Saxon origin. Cockley Cley was originally part of a cluster including All Saints, St Mary and St Peter, the last destroyed in Elizabeth I's reign.

These clusters of churches could have arisen as early monastic settlements for it is known that Celtic monasticism often took the form of group communities dwelling under hermit-like conditions. Each monk or group of monks possessed some sort of church, dedicated it and, as communities grew, the group became a focal point while the cluster remained unquestioned. It should be remembered that the manorial system took hold late in East Anglia though it was thoroughly established by the time of Domesday Book, 1086. Nevertheless communal characteristics of Saxon organisation remained unaltered under Danish occupation

41

Newton by Castle Acre All Saints. Saxon cruciform. Note narrow east tower arch with plain imposts. Under the tower was the sacrarium.

so that there grew up communities of small settlements interdependent within the larger groupings.

Evidence seems to point to the north west corner of Norfolk as having been a possible launching pad for Celtic missionary work in East Anglia. There the remains of the monastic cluster are common. Recently the exposure of ruins of a tripartite Saxon church from beneath earthworks at Castle Rising castle adds yet more evidence. The Babingley river was then a deep water creek and what more possible than that on both sides would have been found settlements. This church was built of Roman stone some of which still shows Roman plaster adhering to it. The apse windows are double splayed slits without quoins, similar in many ways to

St Mary at Cockley Cley. It has been estimated that by A.D. 700 there were over fifty stone churches in England. Bearing in mind that East Anglia was probably the most thickly populated part of the country, some at least of its churches could probably have been built of stone from Roman ruins. Remember that St Dunstan was classifying churches as head minsters, middling minsters and lesser minsters. Those with no burial grounds he called field churches.

It was King Alfred who probably initiated the great wave of Saxon building. The church he erected at Athelney to commemorate the defeat of the Danes in A.D. 878 was of standard Byzantine design. Descriptions state that it was founded upon four great piers. It is stressed that this was the first ever to be built in England upon that plan. So this must have been a 'head minster'. However most churches would have been lesser minsters, the central nucleus of which would have been

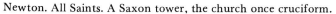

Newton. All Saints. A Saxon tower, the church once cruciform.

the tower with narrow arched openings leading from the nave into north and south porticus and chancel. That King Edgar speaks plaintively of timber is proof that mason craft had still a long way to go. Yet in respect of colour and carving Saxon churches of the period were so lavishly ornamented that they were looked upon as the most decorated in Europe.

Central towers implied transepts or porticus. In a few cases the tower was wider than the nave perhaps to accommodate vestigial ambulatories. Others, not wider than the naves, had the effect of restricting to a narrow corridor the sacrarium space between nave and chancel. It has been suggested that this opening was screened off following a liturgical custom common in the Byzantine rite. At certain stages in the Greek Orthodox Mass today a blind is drawn down on the screen entrance completely shutting off worshippers from the chancel. A possible survival of this earlier Saxon practice was the invariable use in mediaeval England of the Lenten Veil whereby the High Altar and its surroundings were completely shut off by a great curtain of painted linen during the whole of the forty days. The iron roller by which the Veil was raised and lowered can still be seen in the south wall of Ranworth chancel.

There is much in ancient liturgy about which we know nothing and of which we can only surmise from the architectural layout of early churches. Until recently the Latin mass contained the Greek words *Kyrie eleison* and *Christe eleison*. It is not beyond possibility that the Saxon mass was more liberally besprinkled with Greek phrases and probably the whole liturgy was much closer to Greek than to Latin practice. We know that the Greek language was studied in the tenth century monasteries of Saxon England.

In Saxon times England came to be known as the "Ringing Island". Very large bells were cast and hung but how they were rung remains a mystery. We are told that the tones of St Guthlac of Crowland could be heard from afar and were said to cure the headache. At Little Snoring there stands a round detached bell tower. The great beaked arch on its eastern face tells that it was once attached to its church but when, in the second half of the twelfth century another church was built beside it, the tower was maintained for its original purpose.

This and the lofty character of the timber churches brings us to consideration of towers generally. Through the centuries we have come to regard towers as something distinct from and of no intrinsic value to worship, in fact, nothing more than a dominating element in the church complex, a symbolic injunction to look heavenwards. But their original purpose was not so simple. That they are a tradition in church construction is fundamental. We cannot conceive of a mediaeval church without a tower of sorts, whether attached or not. Early builders erected nothing without a purpose and it is often tradition that keeps a device alive after its purpose is fled or has been forgotten. Towers were elements integrated in the one unity. Originally that unity was not a towered church but a tower church and as such was a direct offspring of Byzantium and for centuries was of wood construction.

That the turret church was a commonplace can be proved from study of a twelfth century manuscript, M.736 in the Pierpont Morgan Library in New York. An illustration depicts Edmund being crowned King of the Angles. He is seated within an apse above which rise three turreted churches. They appear to be cruciform, a shape difficult to define in the two dimensional art form of those days, and are surrounded with aisles. The whole seems to be lighted from beneath the turrets. These erections could be the ancestors of lantern towers such as that at East Dereham and Ely. The manuscript, though illumined by monks in St Edmund's Abbey in the twelfth century is mainly by Alban of Fleury (945-1004) and was dedicated to St Dunstan (925-988).

Norfolk has no remaining tower churches. Moreover few centrally planned churches ever were built in England. One was built at Abingdon circa 960 by Abbot Ethelwold and a similarly planned tomb chapel erected at Bury St Edmunds in the eleventh century (1026-1032) to house the shrine of St Edmund, whose cult by then was strong for he was on the way to becoming the patron saint of England. Yet not until the Conquest did French trained Benedictines publicly announce that the centralised plan was unsuitable for a great church. So the long church was gradually forced upon English builders.

On the other hand there is reason to believe that the round towers of East Anglia have stronger architectural associations and closer links with the continent than their present day appearance would suggest. They have to be a subject in themselves. There are 119 in Norfolk, 41 in Suffolk, 8 in Essex and only 12 in all the rest of the country. All are startlingly similar in construction. Their diameters vary from ten feet to 20 feet, their wall thicknesses between two and half feet and five feet. None possesses a staircase, ladders having always been used for access to the upper stages. Some present day ladders could be the originals, heavy, roughly made, their outside members dressed halves of trees sometimes rudely moulded. Their rungs are shaped and carried through the side members at intervals and pinned to prevent spreading. Their length is usually twenty feet.

The majority of Norfolk round towers appear to have been built between 1015 and 1115. They seem not to have been in any way affected by the Norman arrival so it is fair to assume that all these towers, whether pre- or post-Conquest are of Saxon workmanship. Most of our round towers are to be found in the east of the county, a fact that has given rise to at least one of the theories concerning their origin which we shall be discussing later.

Round towers are thought to have been the East Anglian variety of the first Romanesque style of tower which developed in Lombardy in the mid-ninth

Saxon towered Colney St Andrew. No string courses. Small rectangular, double splayed windows North, South and West and a bullseye double splay on West.

Roughton St Mary. Stratified flintwork, carstone, bullseye windows, slits at living level and bifora sound holes all prove the tower Saxon.

century, influence of which spread westwards. Another school of thought maintains that they are more likely due to Carolingian influence emanating from the monastery of St Riquier in Picardy. But the St Riquier towers were staircase and crossing towers and no East Anglian towers were of this type. The nearest of this form of tower is that of All Saints, Brixworth in Northamptonshire. No, if this theory is to hold water then one must assume that it was the shape which impressed East Anglian masons as being a simple method of overcoming a lack of stone for quoins.

Many round towers had no exterior doorways (Bessingham, Colney, East Lexham and Roughton). Some (Bessingham and Colney) had no exterior openings at all but only a door of egress at the second stage in the east wall above the tower arch which could be reached by a ladder from the nave as at Haddiscoe and Roughton. All round towers were built in three stages. Of these the top stage was undoubtedly the belfry, the second stage the ringing chamber and the ground floor a *porticus ingressus,* or porch or, if no external openings existed, just a porticus. This might have served as a vestry, a tomb chamber or indeed might have had a subsidiary altar. On the other hand the floor stage could have been used for secular purposes, fairs, gatherings and perhaps judicial business in the way the south porch came to be used in late mediaeval times.

All our round towers are built of rubble with flint facings. Many preserve evidence of very early work, as for instance tapering, some crude and uneven in quality as at East Lexham. Others reveal great skill in the handling of flint, being finished with stratified or herringbone work and shallow blank arcading as at Tasburgh and Thorpe next Haddiscoe. Kirby Cane is another example where shallow arcading has been worked out in flint. Some towers have string courses, some none at all. Many now have late thirteenth century to fifteenth century octagonal tops that are usually described as belfry stages, giving the impression that it was only when such tops had been added that it was possible to have a ring of bells. Many more have had their original windows replaced with larger ones possessing stone dressings. It is because of a lack of quoining and stone dressing in those still retaining their original features that makes dating them so difficult.

A number of reasons have been advanced for these East Anglian round towers. Cautley, basing his argument on the rude character of much of the work joining tower to nave, suggests that some at least were in situ as defence towers against the Danes and that later the church was added. The presence of so many near navigable waterways and estuaries lends some credence to this theory. But Lincolnshire, that suffered so much more severely from Danish inroads, has no round towers. Furthermore so many towers were built against an existing church, or one contemporary with them, for in these cases their eastern faces are flatter to make easier attachment as, for example, Bessingham. In Colney, Witton and

Bessingham St Andrew. Close-up of bifora, double gabled heads with small stone hoods. Jambs of small stones with lateral strip work, no sills, circular mid-wall shafts with no caps or bases.

Haddiscoe are preserved the three quarter round angle shafts between nave and tower. In others the outer face of the filling is plane, but at Roughton the filling is segmental with the convexity.

An argument has been advanced on slender evidence that the round towers were tower churches such as Fingest in Buckinghamshire. Had the ground floor been vaulted there might have been ground for acceptance of this view but none shows this to have been a practice. J. J. Raven, basing his theory on a law of Athelstan, dated 937 suggests they were Anglo Saxon thegns' bell towers. Some support for this could be found in the fact that the earliest parish priests were the chaplains of Saxon thegns who themselves took deacons' orders to inherit the benefices and tithes of their parishes. It was due to an enduring pre-Conquest tradition that the advowson, or presentation right of a benefice has often continued to remain with the Lord of the Manor throughout the Middle Ages and in many cases down to the present day.

The only sound conclusion for the existence of so many round towers seems to be that, together with the remaining pre-Conquest churches, they were originally built in what were then rich and populous areas but in the thirteenth century, or just after, these areas suffered a loss of population from which they recovered so slowly that the communities were never in a position to change with the times. Even the fifteenth century wealth accruing from the weaving industry seems to have passed them by.

Although the bell tower at the west end of the nave is in many cases a fourteenth or fifteenth century addition, one may yet assume that the England of the eleventh and twelfth centuries, still clinging to a race memory of the Saxon turriform wooden churches, remained a many steepled land and that not only because of the rapidly multiplying monastic houses. The continued existence of an axially planned church of the twelfth century with its central tower but no transepts could be due to the need for incorporating a tower into the design. Additionally there was the economical argument that a central tower could serve three purposes, accommodation for a congregation, dwelling space for a priest and a belfry. There are thirteen centrally towered churches in Norfolk. All possess considerable early work, six are dedicated to St Mary and two to St Andrew. They are Aldeby, Attleborough, Burnham Overy, East Dereham, Flitcham, Fundenhall, Gillingham, Gressenhall, Heacham, South Lopham, Melton Constable, Newton and Great Dunham.

Summing up, the characteristic features of Anglo Saxon workmanship are as follows: pilaster stripwork (such as Lombard bands and blank arcading) banded or plain baluster shafts, the earlier ones cut, the later turned, long and short quoining using in the earliest work uncut fieldstone and later roughly axed material, triangular headed openings, primitive Byzantine *bifora* or openings in bell towers, occuli or round openings, generally double splayed. The true Saxon arches and doorways usually had gone straight through the walls without any knib for the door to shut against whereas recessed rings of orders in arches indicate Norman influence. There are in Norfolk 56 churches that reveal one or more of these characteristic Saxon features.

It is as hard to believe from the vestiges left us that the architectural style of the Anglo-Saxons had been the degenerate form of noble developments far away in a great empire as it is to appreciate that their later wooden minsters were the greatest buildings of the age. Theirs was a supremacy that died with them as the thirteenth century emerged. Ever after, England's architectural supremacy was surrendered for ever to the continent.

CHAPTER THREE

The Four Hundred Years of Architectural Adventure

WERE it not for the adulation that has been lavishly showered upon our Norman conquerors by historians past and present, an adulation that has blinded us to the high standards of culture of our Saxon forebears we might begin to understand better the remarkable architectural achievements during the two centuries before the Battle of Hastings. Sir James Murray in his *Evolution of Lexicography* makes the statement that culturally the Normans were about as far behind the people they conquered as were the Romans when they made themselves masters of Greece.

The Saxons were magnificent builders, far better than the Normans, some of whose work was shoddy stuff. Saxon foundations were strong and their mortar little inferior to that of the Romans. Here, however, we must honestly admit that the mortar of Norwich Cathedral is as hard as concrete in some parts. Despite isolated exceptions we have to accept as fact that 1066 was not a watershed but a bridgehead. It carried into the century ahead a culture that had been conquered militarily and politically but which remained intellectually and spiritually superior and unconquered.

The Normans established in England Romanesque architecture in its bleakest, barest but at the same time, most impressive form. To do this they did not, as we have been led to believe, devastate the continent of masons. Across the sea as great a building boom as this country was about to experience was occupying all the available workers in stone. The basic Norman style of architecture and decoration came originally from Southern France, Lombardy and Northern Spain. We accept that William the Conqueror brought with him his master mason and a small skilled group from whom the Saxons learned and upon whose ideas they imposed their own artistry. After all, the Normans came to this country not to civilise but to seize. Consequently they bent the skills of the vanquished to their own ends as can be seen in some of the early work in Norwich Cathedral. So, in reality, it was Saxon artistry that, in the twelfth century, embellished with its own exuberant imagination the bleak, forbidding Romanesque.

Accept this and the Saxon overlap becomes fact. Inherited skills of the parents were passed to succeeding generations. It can be no exaggeration to say that the wonderful workmanship in fourteenth century screens, benches and pew ends was an inherited gift from Saxon ancestors rather than from their conquerors.

Norwich Cathedral: barrel vaulting in the south aisle — bleak, unadorned, Romanesque.

Unfortunately, apart from the Cathedral, Wymondham Abbey, Binham and Thetford Priories, St Mary, Attleborough and Castle Acre Priory Norfolk is poor in major examples of pure Saxo-Norman work, but vestigially what there is, is superb. The north door of St Margaret, Hales, of St Gregory, Heckingham, the great entrance to Norwich Castle, all are magnificent pieces illustrating that diversity of ornament, learned of the wood carver and fixed in imperishable stone by his successor, the sculptor. Running all these close are St John Baptist, Hellington; St Ethelbert, Larling; St Mary Wroxham, while St Mary Haddiscoe possesses over its fine portal a Saxon carving probably representing Pope Gregory I seated within an apse which in form has similarities with a similar effigy in the Cathedral. In both cases the head is good round Saxon rather than Norman aquiline. An interesting point. The Haddiscoe work deserves more careful preservation than it has received so far.

The question may be asked, "Why, if so much of this ornamentation is Saxon inspired, does it not become enflowered in stone until after the Conquest?" The answer is that, except in the great limestone belt, in the north country and in the south west, the Saxon built largely in wood. Infiltration of Norman vigour and organisation brought about a rapid re-building in stone and in Norfolk, flint, and the skill of the carpenter was transferred to the sculptor in stone. The ubiquitous zig-zag or chevron, for example, is clearly of wood carving origin, developed from taking two opposing swings of an axe at the edge of timber to remove what woodmen call a kerf and then continuing all along the edge of the timber until all had become serrated. During the twelfth century the zig-zag evolved into every conceivable kind of variation, beginning to achieve rolls and deep hollows associated with Gothic mouldings of the next century. By that time the work is that of masons rather than of sculptors. We have ample evidence though that the carpenters' skill never died. From twelfth to fourteenth century the carpenter was responsible for doors, roofs and screens and in the fifteenth century for bench ends, benches, pulpits, stalls and roods. His fundamental skill was never lost.

It is not easy to account fully for the richness of design and workmanship that blossomed during the two hundred years following the Conquest. Apart from documentary evidence describing the glory of the Saxon church we have nothing to go upon save the knowledge that it really did exist and that it represented a quality of veneration that later suffered as great a change as did the architecture. In A.D. 1000 it was the contents of the church that were considered its most precious possession. Of prime esteem were relics of the saints, then followed offerings in gold and silver and lastly, the embellishment of the casket, the decoration itself.

The change that followed was due to the vast increase in veneration of the sacraments. It was now the church more than the treasures it contained that became the precious jewel. This changing attitude coincided with the period of

Haddiscoe St Mary. Saxon sculpture over the South doorway possibly depicting Pope Gregory I. Note similarity with the effigy in Norwich Cathedral.

Hales St Margaret. North doorway probably the finest Saxo-Norman work in Norfolk. Could it have once carried colour?

growing refinement in architecture brought about initially by replacement of the heavy two-handed axe with the bolster, a fine, chisel-like tool. It is still possible to see the uneven diagonal slashes made by the axe and compare them with later tooling which ran absolutely vertical and neatly parallel. This change assisted towards the development of architectural rather than sculptural ornamentation. Under these influences, spiritual and material, the church becomes a mute but convincing witness to the harmony of aesthetic and religious efforts in those who planned, built and paid for its building.

It is reasonable at this point, when wealth was making possible a more prodigal use of stone, to reveal the processes involved in producing stone. Freestone was hacked from the quarries in huge lumps and then split into manageable pieces. True freestone is limestone which is found in a line north-east to south-west through Lincolnshire, Northamptonshire, Oxford, Somerset, Devon and Dorset. Along this line lay the mediaeval quarries. So difficult and costly was all overland carriage that in Norfolk the monastic houses preferred to use Caen stone from Normandy eked out with Barnack stone and clunch. Monasteries and cathedrals were continually greedy for freestone and most grudging towards the secular churches. In fact, not until monastic building and maintenance programmes slowed down did the parish church really come into its own with the result that more often it is churches such as St Peter Mancroft, St Stephens and St Andrew in Norwich and Terrington St Clement in North-west Norfolk that depict Late Gothic at its loveliest than it is the monasteries and cathedrals.

The troubled reign of John (1199-1216) marked the end of Byzantine influence. After the Crusades there came a re-orientation of continental sway. The old Benedictine rule lost its hold. Flow of ideas that had emanated from Byzantium via Germany now emerged from Rome via France and in particular Cluny. So faded the shadow of Romanesque that today leaves us with tantalising remnants that bedevil all study of the break occasioned by the Conquest itself. For example there are in Norfolk 56 churches that show real evidence of Saxon work and 112 where the work must be described as Saxo-Norman. In almost every case these 168 churches have dedications that indicate early foundations. Moreover, wherever ornament occurs it is always in Saxon vernacular, bursting with bucolic joy and humour, revealing a naive credulity and an uncomprehending faith.

Before leaving the pure Romanesque we have to admit that ornate west fronts to parish churches of the period are rare in Norfolk. The best example is that of Castle Rising which has interlaced blank arcading and a Franco-Norman wheel window. A similar front now hidden by its later tower is just over the Suffolk border at Westhall. But Saxo-Norman overlap is evident at Gillingham, Attleborough — though this was monastic rather than secular — and South Lopham. Late work can be seen in Walsoken and at Castle Rising.

Thereafter follows that most amazing transformation which hits the observer, however casual he may be. For architecture takes one gigantic stride into the Middle Ages. Suddenly in every branch of life — in action, organisation, technology — there occurs an outpouring of energy. Evidence is still with us in the ruins of vast monastic churches and in our cathedrals, all of them offspring of one of the great epochs of art. It must have had an enormous impact both intellectual and emotional, upon people whose narrow, monotonous lives were rhythmed only by the occupations of the months, who spent much of the year in darkness and in the cramped condition of windowless huts. What must have been the effect of this inconceivable splendour, so much richer then than its vestiges are today which surely overwhelmed them when they entered even the more humble village church.

Forgotten now was the semi-circular arch with its ornamental sculpture work, the stumpy pillars, the stodgy piers. Clerestories became higher and interiors lighter. Round arched Norman windows became taller lancets. Ribbed vaultings, first mounted to support gallery floors, developed into stone ceilings with slender ribs making a pattern upon them — such as can be seen in the thirteenth century chancel of Blakeney St Nicholas. Gothic had arrived.

That there was mental tension and cultural struggle is evident. They can be seen in the south door of Easton St Peter where there is an amazing display of decoration, banded and capped shafts, jambs alive with twisted rope design and a bobbined and chevroned *but pointed arch*. The struggle is even greater at Little Snoring St Andrew where the builders of the south door could not make up their minds. Consequently a much be-chevroned but pointed arch appears between upper and lower half round arches, the upper one being raised to give it a horseshoe effect.

Early English (Early Gothic) represents fundamentally a throwing away of the old static construction where outward thrust of vault or roof was countered by massive walls. This monolithic style began to be replaced by a more dynamic method of thrust against thrust, a new equilibrium where failure of an element led to entire collapse. Success here inevitably created a striving towards greater height, delicate construction and abundant interior light. The buttress became more than just decoration; it had to balance the vaulting thrust.

I think it doubtful whether any continental professional influences directly affected to a great degree our building craftsmen. More likely is it that intelligent, travelled amateurs, such as those taking part in Crusades and pilgrimages, were responsible for introducing new ideas into architecture. Certainly it was the crusading century that witnessed the transition from Saxo-Norman to the beginnings of Gothic.

Except in very small churches where the parish may have failed to increase its population, naves seldom omitted to develop in size. Perhaps most spectacular was the arcade of arches carried on a series of piers or pillars so that, with an aisle, the size of the church came to be increased. The enrichment of these arcades, in particular capitals, imposts and springing of the arches was the work of carvers.

The thirteenth century became suddenly a period for experimentation. For instance it is difficult to account for the sudden elongation of the chancel. From the beginning of the twelfth century it became a permanent feature and remained so for three centuries. Lighted at first by lancets and later by fine traceried windows, these chancels were well constructed. Each had its priest's door in the south wall. One can only surmise that at this time there came about a change of liturgy. Another possibility is that the new chancel enhanced the dignity of the altar by removing it further from the nave. Worshippers saw the altar as a far-off jewel framed within the chancel arch and viewed through the tracery of a screen. In Saxon days the arch had been kept small, emphasising that same mystery. In the twelfth century it had become the proscenium, typified by that at Framingham Earl, St Andrew. But the thirteenth century saw the introduction of the screen that once again restored much of the element of mystery.

Not that naves were neglected. With the development of aisles went hand in hand an enrichment of the tower arch, to me a clear indication of a change in liturgy calling for the tower base to become an important communal part of the church. Noticeably too the west door went out of fashion and remained that way until the fifteenth century. Another important factor was that the interior of the church was becoming attractive as a place of burial for the wealthy. To have a tomb in the chancel constituted a status symbol particularly if it served as an Easter Sepulchre.

Norfolk is rich in Early Gothic churches. Beyond all else in beauty stands West Walton, finer even than Walsoken, built a hundred years earlier. West Walton was probably the work of masons trained at Lincoln. Its round piers with its six or eight detached and banded shafts, its stiff leafed capitals all bear out this assumption. Unique too are the blank arcaded clerestory and the detached clocher. Similar detached clochers were built at Terrington St Clement and at Norwich Cathedral but of the last nothing remains.

Other fine Early Gothic towers in Norfolk are at Tilney All Saints, Walsoken All Saints and King's Lynn St Nicholas. One or two octagon towers of the period remain, notably at Toft Monks and at Old Buckenham. Some suggest they are originally round towers that have become reclad. There is no constructional evidence in support of this.

West Walton's piers are paralleled at Grimston St Botolph (four shafts) and King's Lynn St Margaret (rich thirteenth century base mouldings to the arcade). These are not general, most Early English arcades having drum alternating with

West Walton St Mary: the most beautiful thirteenth century church in Norfolk. Note above the blank arcaded clerestory. The South porch has octagonal buttresses with typical blank lancets and an arch on attached columns and two rows of dog-tooth ornament. The inner door with four engaged columns and caps. *By courtesy of Eastern Counties Newspapers.*

octagonal piers. This is the arrangement at Walsoken, Aylsham, Reymerston and Thornham. Less familiar forms of pier are Quatrefoil or semi-circular foil (Letheringsett St Andrew and Great Massingham St Mary) or with hollows between the foils so deep as to give the impression of detached stafts (Northwold St Andrew, Foulden All Saints, Hilborough All Saints and Didlington St Michael). Arches remain simple, having hollow more often than normal chamfers.

Other noteworthy elements of Early English can be seen in the south porch of Great Massingham St Mary with its open sided arcading and pinnacled buttresses and the lovely chancels of Burgh St Mary next Aylsham, Great

Cressingham St Michael and Wramplingham SS Peter and Paul (all built between 1250 and 1285), and that of Blakeney chancel, mentioned earlier. In the Cathedral there remains only the Chapel of St Catherine (now the Dean's vestry) and the lovely double arch once leading into the Lady Chapel. It now connects with the modern St Saviour's Chapel. Among smaller pieces may be mentioned piscinas in Hardingham St George and Pulham St Mary, both of which have interlaced arches.

Then, too, Norfolk possesses two superb Early English West Fronts at Binham and Great Yarmouth. Though ruined, Binham is breathtaking and of great historical interest as it can be dated before 1244 yet it has bar tracery — not lancets. This style was evolved at Rheims in 1211 and enlarged from two to four light work at Amiens after 1220. So Binham stands between these and Westminster Abbey which was begun in 1245.

Binham St Mary. A detail of the great west font constructed before 1244, probably the first of its style in England.

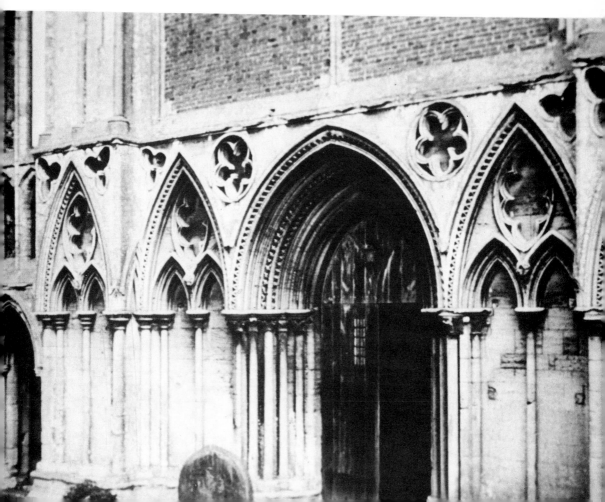

Great Yarmouth St Nicholas claims to be the largest parish church in England. Of thirteenth century work this is true and probably true of the Middle Ages in general. Unfortunately the church was gutted by German firebombs in the Second World War and later rebuilt in an imitation Gothic more European than East Anglian.

New developments in architecture tend always to be written in fenestration and in Early English we find lancets and plate tracery giving place to geometric forms. Plate tracery ends by 1250-60 when geometric forms start and continue until 1320-30. Automatically windows increased in size. Once builders discovered the stability of the mullion their experimentation in geometric and curvilinear tracery knew no bounds and both these developments arose basically from the ogee (⌒) arch. The sculptor, freed from the carver, developed figure sculpture to a high degree, aiming at a perfection lost since classical times. He enhanced the beauty of the pinnacle, gable, buttress and capital with leaf and plant carving, crocket, cusp and ball flower ornament. The west window at Binham represents Geometric tracery at its finest and, as Niklaus Pevsner claims, its purest. He calls it the "paradigm of Geometrical tracery". As the thirteenth century draws to its close fenestration becomes more varied as can be seen in the east window of Trowse Newton St Andrew where quatrefoil appears unencircled and placed diagonally. Also of the last quarter of the thirteenth century are the east windows of North Creake and Carbrooke. The chancel of the former was finished by 1301.

West towers of churches are so common an architectural feature that their progressive refinement in the age of adventure cannot go unnoticed. Refinement can be gauged in a number of ways. There is primarily the question of general mass, the relationship of height to width. According to Munro Cautley the height should be about 3½ times the base width above the plinth. By this standard Winterton, Salle and Norwich St Giles look high, East Dereham and Stalham stumpy. A good base course is an essential feature; Hingham, Cawston and in Norwich, St Peter Mancroft and St Andrews all have splendid base courses.

The division of the tower into stages with string courses was something in which thirteenth century builders excelled and West Walton and Tilney All Saints are proof of this. Buttresses can make or mar a tower; for example the abrupt set-offs below the belfry stage at Salle ruins the tower's appearance. Norfolk builders usually indulged in diagonal buttresses, effective rather than structurally necessary. Among the many, fifteenth century Redenhall is the finest in the county, its great octagonal buttresses string coursed in conformity with the tower and terminating in pinnacles. The use of rectangular buttresses on the tower faces is more rare. These, used within rather than on the edge of the tower walls give an appearance of greater height by presenting additional vertical lines. This last feature is good at North Elmham and Swaffham but too narrow at South Repps, Cromer and Methwold and absent at Cawston.

The crowning glory of a tower is its parapet. In most cases the parapet, if it exists at all is a simple battlemented addition. A few towers only possess lovely parapets, pierced and traceried, as at Hingham, Swaffham and East Harling. At Burnham Market the merlons are carved with figures beneath canopies.

The thirteenth century was the period that popularised Purbeck marble. That it came round the coast by boatload is obvious. Most thirteenth century font bowls in Purbeck marble are to be found near the coast or by navigable rivers, creeks and estuaries and there are 43 in Norfolk. Fonts, bowls, either six or eight sided, were probably rough hewn at the quarry face — areas around ancient quarries in Purbeck have huge heaps of chippings — and there is documentary evidence that marble was not necessarily sent from Corfe in a highly finished state but partially carved. Font bowls were invariably decorated with blank arcading on each face. At its loveliest Purbeck marble can be seen in the remaining banded, detached shafts on the West Walton arcades. Similar detached shafts in Norwich Cathedral cloisters have suffered badly from exposure to the weather for centuries.

As a medium for memorial effigies Purbeck marble gave a shallow effect due to the workable material being never more than between eighteen and twenty-four inches in thickness.

It was Early Gothic that engendered and then ushered in the Decorated (High Gothic) era. The east walk of Norwich Cathedral cloisters was rebuilt from 1297 onwards and the portal from it into the cathedral, called erroneously the Prior's Door, is an exquisite example with artistically sculpted statuettes. Both fenestration and portals of the period are exotic and spectacular. Go and look at Cley. Study its wonderful doorways with their luscious use of cusped and sub-cusped ogee arches. They pale beside the unfinished south transept, a fairy palace of intricate tracery, crocketed gable and finialled and crocketed buttresses. The delicacy of it all forces upon the mind thoughts of Granada and the Alhambra. In fact, recent research has focussed upon the real possibility that Crusaders could have been responsible for bringing from places like Turkey and Morocco ideas that led to the fundamentals of High Gothic.

In lesser degree this decoration can be seen at Ashill, Carbrooke, Elsing and Harpley, and in most of the fenestration of Norwich Cathedral cloisters. The Carnary Chapel in the Cathedral precincts, now Norwich School Chapel, possesses a vaulted undercroft and foiled, cusped and subcusped circular windows. Other less prominent examples in Norwich are the south aisle windows of St Andrew's Hall (once the church of the Black Friars) and its great east window that gazes down Elm Hill. These may well possess the original fenestration plan for the Friars moved from their first home on the north side of the river in 1317. Finally one should include St John Maddermarket, Norwich; Holy Trinity, Ingham, built

Burnham Thorpe. All Saints thirteenth century Purbeck marble font.

Cley St Margaret. Groined fifteenth century porch enclosing fourteenth century cusped and cinquefoiled doorway that looks almost Moorish.

before 1344 as a college of priests; the Slipper Chapel at Houghton St Giles, a mile from Walsingham Shrine; Hilborough, Thompson and the chancel of Worstead St Mary.

Much ornamentation came to be lavished on piscinae, fonts, sedilia and in particular Easter Sepulchres. By 1300 this smaller work, together with delicate figure sculpture, was executed in the great craft shops established in important centres, London for the working of Reigate and Caen stone, Exeter for Beer stone, Norwich for clunch, the pieces being delivered "in the flat" and erected on the spot much as they would be today.

Suddenly, at the very height of this achievement, disaster and devastation hit Western Europe. The Black Death in one generation reduced the population by at least one third. Cultural life came almost to a standstill. Under its impact the existence of the nation staggered. Its interruption to work in progress is apparent all over the country and is evident in Norfolk both at Cley and at Great Yarmouth.

The climate had already played a depressing and mischievous overture to the opera of death. A long decline of temperature had set in, vine growing in England had virtually ceased and following disastrous harvests there were famines in the country in 1272, 1283, 1292 and 1311 and between 1313 and 1319 every country in Europe had lost some two, some three harvests. Lack of sun hindered production of salt so necessary for the winter conservation of meat.

Death had always been a preoccupation with mediaeval man: it now became an obsession with the onset of the plague. He began to see clearly that those set in authority over him were no braver, no wiser and no less vulnerable than he.

The Black Death reached East Anglia in March 1349 and hit the diocese of Norfolk to the extent that great tracts of the country, as for example Breckland, could be said literally never to have recovered. Blomefield records that Norwich, with a population of about 14500 lost over 7000. Only the Fens seem to have been let off lightly. It is fairly certain, however, that the death rate in East Anglia was well above the national average.

When the country emerged from that first and greatest impact of the plague a new conception of art seemed to occur almost overnight. In architecture it was not so much a thoroughgoing rebuilding so much as a recasing of the old styles with a scaffolding of light masonry designed to give the maximum effect with the minimum of labour and expense. That this should be was natural and inevitable for undoubtedly there existed a great shortage of labour after the Black Death and masons, always in demand in the great monasteries, must have been for a time non-existent for any other work. For Royal work masons had to be conscripted. In consequence of these prevailing conditions of labour, many considerable problems of building and extension had to be left to raw and inexperienced tradesmen. This could have brought about the almost universal adoption of Perpendicular (Late Gothic) by the end of the fourteenth century. But in the eastern counties and in particular, Norfolk, masons clung affectionately to the curving patterns of High Gothic. This is what makes the majority of Norfolk churches individual and exciting. Basically similar, there yet exist wide differences in design, in its application and in its arrangement, whether the church be small and primitive or as stately as any the fifteenth century could produce. This affectionate clinging to the curvilinear motif is obvious in the presbytery of Norwich Cathedral, rebuilt in the 1360s and in the nave, the three storeyed porch and in the west tower of Ingham Holy Trinity. Both these establishments being formerly monastic, could command the labour necessary for the work to be completed.

In the absence of general documentation, the chronology of parochial architecture remains of necessity vague. It would appear that a century of dilapidation passed during which many churches were allowed to deteriorate without provision for maintenance while the greater monastic churches continued to absorb most of the country's building potential. Contemporary reports mention this lapse. However, with the increase of wealth from wool following the Black Death, the parish church seems to have taken on a new lease of life.

Like the Cotswolds, Norfolk had come to live upon the sheep's back but, hampered by lack of local stone, it imported small quantities of good quality freestone. This in conjunction with the local flint produced the fretted patterning known as flushwork. Such sumptuous chequer-board patterning in the contrasting blue black of flint and grey white of freestone was worked into designs similar to those used for parapets of the period. Its diversity lends to the exteriors of many Norfolk churches a charm completely lacking where only stone is used. It became the rage in the second half of the fifteenth century perhaps because its exuberance satisfied the Tudor taste for the rich and flamboyant. It is present on buttresses, porches, parapets and base courses. Patterns can be chequer or diaper, the simplicity of mere initials or crowned Ms, or, as in the Thorp chapel, St Michael Coslany, Norwich, walls entirely devoted to tracery motifs paralleling the nearby east window and likened by Blyth in 1842 to "inlaid ivory work of old cabinets." The chancel at Wiveton St Mary with similar imitative flushwork must be some of the earliest in the county, probably about 1320. Next in age are the gatehouse of the Carmelite Priory of Burnham Norton and the panelled battlements of Elsing St Mary tower. Equal in quality with all these are the big polygonal buttresses of the tower of Redenhall St Mary, near Harleston.

Lack of stone early turned the attention of Norfolk builders to another medium, that of brick, imported at first from the Netherlands. By the second quarter of the fifteenth century bricks were being made locally and their use may be seen in the perfection of Shelton St Mary, one of the finest Late Gothic

Norwich. St Michael Coslany. The remarkable flushwork of the south aisle and east font.

churches in the county. It was rebuilt in brick with stone facings by Sir Ralph Shelton who died in 1497. The soft brick, mellowed to maroon, is diapered with dark blue headers while the clerestory of nine windows, so close set as to appear as one, are faced with ashlar.

There are four visible stages in the East Anglian use of flint. All Norfolk is familiar with its use as rubble, in walls or as the core of piers and pillars. The second stage is gained by splitting the flint nodule to give a clean but irregular surface. This never became common, though in Victorian times it was revived in imitation Gothic work. Knapping came next, a method of chipping the flint to a preconceived shape. Early flushwork exhibits a great amount of knapping. Perfection was achieved when the cutting of flint was developed. Flushwork of Norwich Guildhall

66

and the walls of the home of William Appleyard, first Mayor of Norwich, built in 1370, now known as the Bridewell Museum are among the many perfect examples of this work.

The early and mid fourteenth century, the era of the Edwards I, II and III, wealthy, realistic and progressive, was the period of the great preaching naves. They were copied from the Friars' churches. In Norfolk it resulted in the spacious hall churches that can be seen around the coast from the Wash to Great Yarmouth and inland at Fakenham, Swaffham, Salle and Norwich, to name but a few. In many ways these reveal the change from exuberant High Gothic to the more austere, subtle, clean lined Late Gothic or Perpendicular. Nevertheless it is necessary to keep well in mind the overlap of the two styles. As already stated the clerestory of Norwich Cathedral presbytery was rebuilt in the 1360s, Terrington

Norwich S. Peter Mancroft. Hammer beam roof, the hammers coved and vaulted as in a rood screen.

St Clement and Worstead around 1380 and Cawston prior to 1414. Their size, their slender piers and wide aisles, or their naves without aisles mark the tendencies that existed throughout the fourteenth and fifteenth centuries. During this time High and Late Gothic fenestration motifs appear side by side. This parallelism is evident in a number of Norwich churches, notably St George Tombland, St Gregory and St John Maddermarket. In the county Belaugh St Peter, Catfield All Saints and Walcott All Saints show the same lack of desire to change the old ways.

Features of Norfolk Perpendicular can now be classified. Clerestories are unusually tall and in character almost continuous as at Shelton St Mary. Battlements and parapets are not frequent except as finials of a tower for the East Anglian always showed preference for a high pitched roof. After a century of neglect wood has again assumed prominence as a medium both for the elaborate ornamentation of fine hammer beam roofs and for screens and roods, for pulpits and for benches and bench ends. Whether or not the chancel arch remained — in the majority of cases it did — the screen became an imposing feature of all interiors. It was the period when veneration of the rood reached its peak. Elaborate rood screens with rood lofts above were the outcome. We have only to study the exquisite work in the Ranworth St Helen screen, the lovely painted panels of Cawston St Agnes and Tunstead St Mary, of Ludham St Catherine and Barton Turf St Michael to realise that the humblest of parish churches that today may perhaps possess only the rood stair once leading to the loft, could have cherished an equally imposing feature. For example Holme Hale St Andrew still has a beautiful screen with ogee headed one light divisions and much fine tracery including two of rose window type in the spandrels of the entrance.

There exist indications that in some parochial churches the upper part of the chancel arch was blocked or covered over with a boarded tympanum painted to act as a backcloth to the rood. Often it depicted a doom or judgement. At Ludham St Catherine it takes the form of a Crucifixion which may be of Maryan origin. Yet, rich as Norfolk is in remains of fine screens there are in existence few Celures — Canopies of Honour — above the rood. Possibly wholesale restoration of roofs has brought about their disappearance. The best remaining celures with colour are at Cawston St Agnes and Pulham St Mary Magdalen and there is an uncoloured one at Great Witchingham St Mary.

So we have reached the final mediaeval glory, Norfolk's wealth of Late Gothic churches. They represent the achievement of faith married to prosperity for ultimately it was wealth that made possible the attraction of masons, carpenters and sculptors away from the great monastic foundations. Granted their main building programmes were mainly over by c. 1300, yet upkeep of monastic establishments still entailed a constant demand. So we see here a conflict in which secular wealth was already winning. Still another factor making possible the magnificence of Late Gothic (Perp.) was the greater availability of good freestone. By the fifteenth century it could be bought on the quay side at Great Yarmouth. So, with material and skill to hand there arose churches that must have shone amid their drab mediaeval surroundings. There is an element of pride about their towers. Cromer is 160 feet, North Walsham was originally 147 feet, Hingham and St Giles, Norwich 120 feet. Apart from the Cathedral some have spires of which Snettisham is a noble example. In other cases towers are capped with fleches or spirets.

I think it probable that the tragedy of the Black Death was spiritually responsible for the change from High Gothic exuberance to the austerity of Late Gothic. On the other hand it can be argued that we had, prior to 1350, a style emanating from the great monastic houses and now, diversion of professionals from monastic workshops to parochial work led to a type of mass production and an element of streamlining in the work produced.

Considerable doubt is now cast upon the theory that the Black Death was in part responsible for the apparent sudden transition from the florid exuberance of High Gothic (Decorated) architecture to the comparative austerity of Late Gothic (Perpendicular) with its rigid verticals and horizontals. Actually the essential features of the new style, which are related to the reticulated pattern of former years, were in being fifteen years before the onset of the pestilence. The process is one by which reticulation is compressed so that each tends to develop straight vertical sides instead of continuous curves. This is first seen in the work of William Ramsey on the south cloister of Norwich Cathedral in about 1324 and in the new cloisters and chapter house of old St Paul's Cathedral on which he worked in 1332.

Inspiration probably emanated from the east. During the early thirteenth and fourteenth centuries something akin to the 'compressed' hexagons of Perpendicular tracery is reported as seen in Muslim buildings in Egypt. This characteristic is described in the itinerary of two Franciscans, Simon Simeon and Hugh the Illuminator who went to the Holy Land in 1323. Their narrative first belonged to Simon Bozoun, Prior of Norwich in 1344-52.

The word Perpendicular describing the period is perhaps the happiest and most helpful as far as the reader is concerned. In fenestration it immediately solves any difficulty of recognition. Mullions are vertical to the first order of the window arch. The many mullions, and in larger window, transoms, break up the vast areas of glass and make easier the pictorial use of stained glass, which, by the fifteenth century was contributing largely to the 'teaching picture' character of the church.

In arcades, porches and doorways arches become wider and less pointed. Pillars are lofty, slim and with the slightest of capitals. Often arches run their mouldings right down into the pillars without any indication of a springing line and then only the inner mould will carry the smallest of caps. In fact the weakest

Tunstead St Mary. The rood beam still in position above the screen.

item of Late Gothic ordinance is its failure to agree on the form of the capital. The Corinthian, that had filtered down through the centuries and was now far from home had, until the Late Gothic, retained its three characteristics, the abacus or impost moulding, the spreading bell and the astragal or joint separating it from the shaft. In the fifteenth century all merged into one, leaving only the heavy cove that lingered on as long as masonry mouldings survived.

We are still very much in the dark regarding the way in which the liturgy of the church was organised even as late as the fifteenth century. In many cases the long chancel remained, its mystery enhanced by a richly carpentered and painted screen. Was the chancel kept long because it had become the last resting place of many of the local nobility? Frequently low arched recesses reveal early interments; sumptuous recesses contain effigies such as that of Sir William Gerbrygge and his wife in Wickhampton St Andrew and of Sir Robert de Bois — a coloured wooden effigy — in Fersfield St Andrew. By the time the fifteenth century had dawned many a local bigwig had built his family chapel, an example of which is the Thorp chapel in Ashwellthorpe All Saints which contains what is the finest alabaster tomb in the county, that of Edmund de Thorp and his lady. Favoured burial positions were the north side of the chancel where a table tomb might serve as a later Easter Sepulchre. The pretentious redstone Morley tomb (1435) in Hingham St Andrew was undoubtedly used for this purpose as well as the more humble table tomb in the south chancel of Tasburgh St Mary.

Popularity of the sermon introduced a new element in worship and some fifteenth century painted chalice pulpits remain to prove this assertion. Those in South Creake St Mary, Salle, SS Peter and Paul and South Burlingham St Edmund

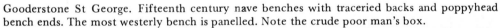

Gooderstone St George. Fifteenth century nave benches with traceried backs and poppyhead bench ends. The most westerly bench is panelled. Note the crude poor man's box.

are outstanding. It could be that a result of this popularity of preaching was the introduction of fixed seating in the naves. Not until the late fourteenth century was there any form of seating for the congregation other than low stone benches by the walls or around the pillars as at Tunstead St Mary and Little Dunham St Margaret.

This introduction of fixed seating presented a new opportunity for the joiners, carpenters and carvers and Norfolk is particularly rich, having 117 churches with mediaeval benches or remains of them. Undoubtedly the best of them are to be seen at the Wiggenhalls in North-west Norfolk, at Bressingham St John the Baptist and at Forncett St Peter. The bench end died out with the Renaissance when pews came to be framed up in a sophisticated style and the ends reduced to mere panelled frames.

With the Reformation came the end of church building for a century or more and the army of masons, carpenters and the like transferred their allegiance from the church to the great and powerful landowners who were demanding mansions ostentatious enough to demonstrate their wealth. In a wave of austerity opposing papistry and all its works, artistry, colour and light were driven from interiors of churches and they began to wear something of the cold appearance they have today.

Summing up the local scene of this great period of architectural impetus it could be true to say of Norfolk that it is a hotch potch. The county must have been one of great density of population judging by the number of villages. Cautley in 1949 spoke of there being 659 churches built prior to 1700, 65 new or rebuilt since that date and 245 ruined churches. Areas such as north Norfolk that enjoyed wealth straight off the sheep's back produced such marvels as Walpole St Peter, Terrington St Clement, Salthouse St Nicholas, Blakeney St Nicholas, Cromer SS Peter and Paul and, inland, Gooderstone St George and Salle SS Peter and Paul where, generally speaking, the work is mainly fifteenth century. Further east and south wealth flowed in from weaving the wool and the story is repeated at North Walsham St Nicholas, the south porch of Worstead St Mary, Tunstead St Mary and the Norwich churches of St Andrews, St Stephen, St Peter Mancroft and St Michael Coslany. Beyond these that in reality were industrial areas of enormous wealth, were the scores of tiny hamlets and villages whose churches were always of the make-do and mend type. If they possessed patrons of wealth and faith their churches retained an air of past grandeur, like Elsing St Mary or Ringland St Peter. Otherwise we find the church embodying bits and pieces that reveal a general and continuous poverty trying hard to keep up with the times with refenestration here and there, an added aisle or an additional storey to the tower. Fundamentally little alteration came to be made to the centuries old rubble walls of their fore-fathers other than keeping the place moderately water-tight.

CHAPTER FOUR

The Great Divide — 1538 to 1974

THE reformation that weakened the hold of Rome upon western Europe was in England more constitutionally effective. This was due in part to the anti-clericalism of a people tired of the predominance of priests yet not wholly converted to a new religion. It was carried forward to success by the greed of king and courtiers to which was added the pride of a people grown conscious of its nationhood and no longer content to be governed in spiritual matters from Italy and Spain.

Violent revolution in life and thought in any age unfortunately brings in its train wanton destruction and the church offered ample opportunity for vandalism and desecration. Being more political than liturgical the English Reformation revolved around a conflict for power and money. The Dissolution of the Monasteries, chantries and gilds was not sufficient to satisfy these so king and government must pillage the rich heritage of the church. Here the incentive preached was papistical usage and the king's sequestrators made full use of it. Perhaps humble rural churches came to escape the full force and fury of the reformers though all suffered more or less. Great Witchingham accounts tell us that, as early as 1538, all lights except that over the Rood were doused. Henry VIII, who afore-time had worshipped barefoot at the shrine of Our Lady of Walsingham, personally ordered the removal of the image and saw that it was publicly burned at Smithfield. He followed this with the enforcement of his order enjoining that " . . . such images as had been abased to superstition be taken out."

His successors, Regents to the boy king Edward VI, quickly turned on the reformatory heat. In 1547 they ordered that " . . . all images whatsoever should be taken out of the churches" and that they remove " . . . all shrines, tables, candle-sticks, trindalls or rolls of wax, pictures, paintings and other monuments of feigned miracles so that no memory of them remain." As in every age, vandals were eager and willing to hasten the destruction.

This destruction and spoliation of what was beautiful, the craftsmanship of ages, and the wiping out in many cases of the accumulated knowledge of centuries had its equal only in earlier tragedies, like the burning of the Library at Alexandria. As Dr Augustus Jessop wrote in *Before the Great Pillage*, "The day will come when someone will write the story . . . of the miscreants who robbed the monasteries . . . and of the ring of robbers who robbed the poor and helpless in the reign of Edward VI." In Norwich alone 12 hospitals, 38 hermitages, 22 chantries and 37 gilds disappeared. John Bale, the antiquary, tells of a merchant who bought two libraries for waste paper and they lasted him ten years.

Desecration took place, not only in things material. It affected men's minds and thoughts. Habits centuries old were rooted out with abandon. Institutions essential to the community were discarded. Schools went because the pupils prayed for their founders. Homes for the old were closed for similar reasons and their Bedesmen swelled the concourse of Tudor vagrants and beggars for whom Poor Laws had to be passed. Gilds to protect the wayfarer, feed, warm and give him a bed, all went in the general holocaust. Even the church's right to grant sanctuary, instituted by Alfred the Great, was denied by Henry VIII.

An official inventory of church goods soon followed. Things were disappearing too fast for the official mind, so parishes were ordered not to part with anything or to remove goods "to their own gain". When the final plundering began in 1553 the Commissioners were empowered to leave only sufficient for conduct of the Divine Service. This they generally interpreted as one bell — the smallest — and one chalice, and they sold all copes, altar cloths, vestments and metal and brought in " . . . all ready money, plate and jewels certified to remain." The churchwardens of St Lawrence, Norwich, paid "three shillings and sixpence for taking down the old perk", meaning the rood. We suppose they handed over the balance on the sale of the wood.

An example of the Commissioners' thoroughness can be seen in the inventory at Knapton. The church housed eight guilds: it possessed a silver gilt cross weighing 31 oz. and a chalice of 9 oz. also numerous vestments of satin, damask and velvet richly decorated and embroidered in gold. There were three bells one weighing ten cwt., one 7 cwt. and one 5 cwt. There were candelsticks, a pair of 'standards' and a number of small ones for processional purposes. The Commissioners had the lot leaving only the chalice and the 5 cwt. bell to help out the Divine Services.

Surely now there would be little left to destroy other than the bare fabric of the church itself. Not so. In some way or another sections of the population that had no love for the new faith, managed to hide some of the treasures of their church that, for them, were part of life itself. Ludham's screen came to be hidden with a high pew. One fears that later, when Mary brought back the ancient faith, they flaunted their possessions. Where a few years earlier, destruction had been wholesale, on her accession, roods were quickly restored and an old writer remarked that "the carvers and makers of statues had a quick trade". At many a church, as for instance Ludham St Catherine, the order was met by painting the rood on a tympanum above the chancel arch.

With the Roman Church busy cleansing its own Augean stable who knows what might have happened in England had Mary's counter reformation borne less cruel an aspect? The horrors of persecution, the torturing and burning, put additional weapons in the hands of the reformers and hardened the disrespect felt generally for the old faith. So Elizabeth I found it easy to re-enact earlier orders regarding articles of superstitious usage and this time they were not only removed but destroyed. Stone altar tables (mensas) were smashed or desecrated — you walk upon three in the flooring of Terrington St Clement — and all rood lofts taken down to the top of the vaulting. Then it was that the lovely painted figures on Ranworth screen were daubed with pitch. She ordered that a "decent table" standing on a frame, be provided for the Communion. This order accounts for the many fine Elizabethan and Stuart tables — nearly 200 — being used for that purpose in the county. Lovely examples can be seen at Great Bircham St Mary, Beeston Regis All Saints, South Acre St George, Castle Acre St James and Walsoken All Saints.

It must be remembered that the Eastern Counties were by this time in the

Norwich St Helens. An early Stuart table.

vanguard of the Puritan movement. By the early seventeenth century Puritanism was to speak with a powerful voice in both spiritual and political affairs. One would expect that this reformatory zeal would have swept clean the house. In most cases it did, but there remained pockets of conservative thought and action that once more hid their treasures and concealed the facts regarding them. Font panels were plastered over as at Hemblington All Saints and Gresham All Saints. Many a secret recess has revealed hidden mediaeval articles that should have been destroyed.

All church building, even necessary repair work ceased for where was the incentive to keep alive bare walls when all their beauty was gone? It was indeed difficult in that dead century, 1550-1650 to keep alive a semblance of orthodox worship for people had now to be fined a shilling a Sunday for non-attendance at church. During the two decades before the Commonwealth Revolution Archbishop Laud made efforts to restore a measure of sanctity into church interiors. Plain glass filled the windows, communion rails fenced in altars, now restored to the east end, and walls were decorated with "goodly sentences" in dismal black Gothic script.

Puritanism in power put the finishing touches to destruction. Theirs was the third desecration. Men like Dowsing, designated Parliamentary Visitors, did their worst and conscripted the hooligan breed to assist them. Lovely hammer beam roofs lost their angelic adornments, fonts were either removed or hacked beyond recognition. Worst destruction of all was to the remnants still remaining of mediaeval glass. Dowsing in his diary refers to upwards of 150 churches in East Anglia where glass was smashed and nearly 7,000 "superstitious pictures" he ordered to be destroyed. Though far from dead the ancient faith was now completely dispossessed of all material wealth.

What can the Norfolk church of today show of this blank, uninteresting period? Only those things that then contributed to the act of worship which could be contained in the phrase "The Preaching of the Word". The county has many seventeenth century pulpits, some single decker, some two or three decker, the last intended to accommodate in descending order the parson, the clerk and the precentor. Some, as at Tibenham All Saints still possess an ornate tester, or sounding board. Others, as at Merton St Peter, have the hour glass beside the pulpit. Most carved work of the period conforms to a decadent art pattern of panels embodying low relief classical arches and false perspective. At Salle the fifteenth century chalice pulpit has been incorporated into a seventeenth century three decker while at Burlingham St Edmund the pre-Reformation pulpit has achieved a seventeenth century tester.

The architectural and artistic decrepitude of the church fabric could lead to the assumption that people's interest in God was practically as dormant. The

Salle: fifteenth century pulpit changed to a three decker of the seventeenth century type with a back board and tester.

opposite was only too true. Never in its history had the Englishman talked more about religion and about God. By the time of the Commonwealth in 1649 he shouted his religion in public places, in battle, in business, in the home and everlastingly in Parliament. The Bible, full stops, commas, mistranslations was free to all who could read and for all to make their own interpretations on the scriptural texts. Out of this welter of obstreperous dogmatism arose the Fifth Monarchy men, the Millenarians, the Muggletonians, the Seventh Day Baptists among the lesser fry of the Commonwealth sects. The Independents, now called Congregationalists, the English Presbyterians, now mostly Unitarians, the Baptists and Quakers were among the greater sects. Norfolk had them all and they in turn helped develop the Meeting House.

Of church building there was none until after the Restoration of the Monarchy and the Great Fire of London in 1666. The Wren churches were entirely Metropolitan. Fifty years were still to pass before Norfolk came to show Wren's influence at work. North Runcton All Saints, attributed to Henry Bell, was built between 1703 and 1713. Great Yarmouth St George, by John Price, 1714-16, of brick with stone facings, is perhaps even more typical an example of Classical revival at work with its pedimented doorway and its tall Tuscan pilasters. The little church of Gunton St Andrew, designed by Robert Adam in 1769 is more a private chapel but it calls for mention because it is again in pure Classical tradition with its Tuscan columned portice and its delicate interior with fluted Corinthian columns and pilasters.

Wren's original design for St Pauls was the outward and visible embodiment of the Protestant church with emphasis on preacher and congregation. Court influence obliged him to discard this and to work upon the Greek Cross project far remote from "Gothic rudeness". His smaller churches have a strikingly Nonconformist character. There were galleries, people sat in pews and the services were conducted from a three decker. And this is the picture we get of the Old Meeting House in Colegate, Norwich, built in 1693 when the persecution of Nonconformists following the Restoration of 1661 had died down. Six years later the Friends' Meeting House in the Gildencroft was built. By 1754 the wealthy weavers and throwsters of Norwich who, a century earlier had established a Presbyterian Meeting House in Colegate, decided to rebuild. The result was the Octagon Chapel, by Thomas Ivory, a building that clearly illustrates how thoroughly the Palladian influence had soaked down into local architectural thinking.

The year 1711 saw the Act of the Fifty New Churches. The effect of this was again Metropolitan and now Hawksmoor was the presiding arch-architect. For all that, desecration number four, the awful neglect of the eighteenth century was gripping the Established church, none more so than in the Diocese of Norfolk, later to be known as the "Dead See".

Colby is but one example out of many of what could happen during this disastrous period. Within the space of three years, 1748-50, the north aisle was taken down and replaced by a brick wall. Lead from the roof was sold to pay for this "restoration". In the course of the work memorial slabs, tomb chests, brasses and heraldic glass from the windows, all mentioned as being in situ a few years earlier by Blomefield, just disappeared.

Though typical of an attitude of indifference, conditions in a rural area such as Norfolk could have affected national policy but little in those days. Instead it was the hapless state of the great industrial towns of the north which, but for the ministrations of Wesley and his followers would have had no spiritual guidance at all.

However, not until 1811 did the national conscience arouse itself sufficiently for a Church Building Commission to be set up. In 1818 Parliament finally acted on its findings. From then until 1856 there were passed thirty-eight Church Building Acts. They caused an outcry from long established and wealthy congregations because, indirectly through the Church Rates, they were being made to pay for the furnishing and maintenance of new churches by having their own grants reduced. Moreover the parish could be liable for the cost of church repairs for twenty years. As far as Norfolk was concerned, the effect of all this was minimal. Where Norwich had expanded beyond its ancient walls the Acts helped. Christ Church, New Catton, by John Brown, was built 1841-2 and St Marks, Lakenham in 1844 by the same architect. Right at the end of the period came St Matthew, Rosary Road, an essay in Romanesque, again by the ubiquitous John Brown in 1851. Yarmouth's expansion, that much slower, called for little church building, St Peter, St Peter's Road, by J. J. Scoles 1831-3, St Mary, Southtown Road, 1831-2 by the same architect and St John, York Road by J. H. Hakewell, right at the end of the period. King's Lynn, untouched by development at that time, had only one new church, St John the Evangelist, built by Salvin in 1846.

The effect of the Acts on existing ancient churches and on their fabrics and furnishings was diabolic, particularly in Norfolk. Because Gothic was then a dirty word, destruction proved easier and more economic than any form of artistic restoration. Granted a faculty had, then as now, to be obtained for any alteration to church fabric or furnishings but a faculty was no open sesame to profundity of knowledge or to any quality of aesthetic judgment. So any enlightened church opinion was powerless to prevent abominable changes made in the name of restoration. According to Cautley in his *Norfolk Churches*, of the 660 mediaeval churches only 172 now retain their ancient roofs, a small number compared with other counties. With destruction of roofs went also priceless examples of wood craftsmanship in screens, benches and pulpits, seating often being replaced with execrable pitch pine.

Happily a change was not far off; light was visible even though this era of mediocrity had not spent itself. In 1833 Augustus John Northmore Pugin was to become the artistic leader of the English Gothic Revival. His evangelistic attitude stemmed the tide of disorderly Graeco-Roman-*Gothick* abortions that were a characteristic of the second and third decade of the nineteenth century. At first his was a predilection for the Gothic stemming from the eighteenth century and not till later did he reveal his preference for fifteenth century Perpendicular (Late Gothic) as being best suited to the requirements of his time. He, together with Ruskin, led the great Ecclesiological reaction that made possible any real development.

Norfolk, always fifty years behind any large Metropolitan movements, felt the first impact of the Gothic revival in the 1870s. In Norwich, Christ Church, by Brown and Pearce, was built in 1873, St Philips, by Edward Power, about the same time and St Thomas, by Ewan Christian in 1886. Most important of all the city's churches of the period was St John's Roman Catholic church (1884-1910) by George Gilbert Scott Junior and, when he died, by his brother, John Oldred Scott. At the time it was the largest revived Gothic Church built in England for Roman Catholics and, apart from its apsidal Lady Chapel can be described as a most perfect example of native Early English.

In the county only the little village of Booton can be said to possess an example of the period, a lavish little extravaganza begun in 1875 and finished in 1891. Built to the design of the rector, the Rev. Whitwell Elvin, it has been described by Niclaus Pevsner as designed with knowledge of Early English but with a happy disregard of its principles. The diagonal placing of the two west towers is more typical of 1820 than of 1890.

At this point it becomes necessary to return to the years following the Reformation in order to follow up another important thread in the pattern of church building, that of Nonconformity. By the time of the accession of the Stuart dynasty to the Throne in 1603, the Puritans had become a living force in the country's religious life and were to remain so for the next three hundred or more years. Through suffering and persecution Puritanism grew in strength. Quakers, Baptists, Presbyterians, Unitarians, Congregationalists and later, Methodists all had a history of hardship and each in turn has made a major contribution to our present concept of religion. Combined they represent one of the great revolutionary movements of mankind, capable of enlarging men's minds, transforming the humblest labourer into one willing to suffer torture and death for the principles of freedom of conscience. Not for nothing did Latimer cry out to Ridley as the flames crackled around them, "Be of good cheer. Play the man. We shall this day light such a candle, by God's grace in England, as I trust shall never be put out." Unfortunately it has to be said that, while democratic in theory and organisation, the Puritans were intolerant of all who differed from their views in practice.

When some years after the Restoration of the Monarchy in 1661 chapels came to be built without any particular reasons for secrecy, the desire was strong to reject any symbolic association with the Established Church. The aim was to have preaching houses where the congregations were direct participants rather than observers of ritual. But by the eighteenth century Nonconformity and Dissent were no longer sheet anchors of the poor alone. They often included the wealthy, educated industrialist and their chapels were of the highest order of architecture. In this respect mention must again be made of the Old Meeting House (Independent) and the Octagon Chapel (Presbyterian) in Colegate, Norwich. Both were built in fashionable styles and lavishly furnished. Of the latter Wesley commented in 1757, " . . . The inside is finished in the highest taste and is as clean as any gentleman's saloon. The communion table is fine mahogany; the very latches of the pew doors are polished brass. How can it be thought that the old coarse gospel should find admission here?"

In the nineteenth century chapel building became a mania and few villages today are without one or two examples. Not that they dominate the landscape as they do in many a northern town and Welsh village. Norfolk has no soot blackened Pennine Salems and Bethesdas. Yet in most villages stands a chapel embracing a central porch flanked with round headed windows remarkably reminiscent of the earliest Saxon churches and as recognisable of its period as Early English or Perpendicular. Yet architecture had little or nothing to do with them.

At this stage mention can only be made of a few outstanding examples of Nonconformist meeting houses of the period in question: in Norwich, Calvert Street Methodist 1810 (now destroyed), Princes Street Congregationalist 1869 by Boardman and St Mary's Baptist Church by Stanley Wearing (the present building is the third on the site, the first being built in 1744). Yarmouth's Central Hall was originally a Congregational Chapel built in 1850. The Methodist Temple, Priory Plain, 1875, was a vast affair, its enormous facade with attached giant pilasters and a steep allover pediment dominating the area. King's Lynn, between 1841 and 1860 saw four chapels built. At the turn of the century, rapidly expanding coastal holiday resorts such as Hunstanton, Sheringham and Cromer found it needful to enlarge their existing modest chapel accommodation.

The keynote of most village chapel interiors is simplicity, a meeting house for corporate worship. Smell is the arresting feature — smell of pine varnish and wax polish. Varnished woodwork, distempered walls, polished brass, red pew carpets or cushions, velvet pulpit frontals and piles of hymn books materially contribute to the atmosphere. Any existing blank wall arcade will have a ribbon of texts in Gothic stencilling.

Norwich. The Old Meeting House, Colegate. 1693.

Except in Quaker meeting houses the pulpit occupies the focal point. The Minister's chair is usually a good one (see Cromwell's brother's chair in the Old Meeting House, Norwich). At first the pulpit had an hour glass but by the late eighteenth century there would be a clock facing the minister. The pews were designed for simplicity and uniformity rather than for comfort. In the little Presbyterian chapel at Hapton, erected 1750, seats in the galleries and in the "horse box" pews beneath are of bare scrubbed wood and are only eight inches wide — with straight up backs.

Hymn singing, always a congregational feature, was originally led by a precentor with a pitch pipe. Later in the nineteenth century organs or harmoniums became common. It was the vigorous, almost tempestuous, strongly evangelical hymn singing that gave Nonconformists, particularly those of the Methodist persuasion the name of "ranters". In the latter half of the nineteenth century the hymnody of American evangelists, in particular Moody and Sankey, strongly influenced the liturgy of Nonconformity.

For the last time we return to the seventeenth century to trace the story of the dispossessed Roman Catholics in Norfolk. Though despoiled of fortunes and chattels, tortured and burnt for their faith, the Catholics bore out the axiom that persecution always strengthens any righteous cause. The story of two hundred years is one of ferocious hatred of anyone or anything savouring of popery. When they could the Roman Catholics fought back. For example, local gentry who were recusants — those who refused by reasons of faith to attend the orthodox church — often allowed the parish church to become ruinous to prevent its being used at all. Bowthorpe, Costessey, Easton, Earlham, Runhall and Stanninghall suffered in this respect. At Costessey and Kimberley means were provided for the celebration of the Mass in secret chapels — in the former house the chapel was in the attic. Not until 1819 was the Chapel of St Augustine built in the grounds of Costessey Park.

Norwich. The Octagon Chapel, Colegate. 1756.

In 1595 Father John Walpole of Norfolk, after fourteen times being tortured in the Tower, was executed at York. The Venerable Robert Southwell, S. J. born at St Faiths, was hung, drawn and quartered at Tyburn. In Norwich, in 1616, this was the fate of Father Thomas Tunstall. He suffered a martyr's death at Magdalen Gate and his head was exhibited on St Benedict's Gate.

Despite ferocious persecution the Jesuits, from 1650 onwards, retained a hold upon Norfolk. They founded a chapel and hall in 1687 between the river and St Andrews Plain in Norwich which was destroyed by rioters a year later. Nevertheless they remained.

Although the Emancipation Act of William and Mary, 1689, gave comparative freedom to Nonconformists, Roman Catholics and Unitarians were still excluded from living as members of a free society. A few years later the Jesuits built another chapel near to Chapel Field and there they remained until 1760. Wealthy Catholic families such as the Jerninghams at Costessey were able to harbour priests who, in their efforts to maintain missionary work, came and went like ghosts. It is an interesting point that the Jerninghams received unlooked-for help from Cromwell. A letter from him is extant ordering the soldiers to refrain from visiting Costessey Park during their investigations.

In 1760-1 the Jesuits established a chapel in St Swithins, Norwich with a secret passage to it from St Benedicts, always guarded by sentinels. By 1773 the Catholics had twelve chapels and twelve priests in East Anglia.

Despite sporadic action by mobs, conditions slowly improved. Immediately following the Catholic Relief Act of 1791 the Jesuits bought land in St John Maddermarket, Norwich and built the church of St John the Baptist — it is now the Maddermarket Theatre. The priests' home was next door, a large mediaeval house known as the Stranaers' Hall which remained their presbytery until 1880.

The Catholic Emancipation Act of 1829 at last brought full freedom of thought and action to all, including the Unitarians who, having helped sponsor the Act, slipped in a clause ensuring their own complete emancipation. At once, following this freedom the Catholics prepared to build Willow Lane Chapel in Norwich, by John Leadbetter, S. J. Its fine Palladian entrance was proof that the Catholics had become openly accepted into a strongly Low Church and Puritan society. In 1881 the Jesuits quietly handed over presbytery and chapel to the Bishop of Northampton and left Norwich, their mission ended.

The foundation stone of St John the Baptist church, about to be built outside St Giles's gate on the site of the old city jail was laid in 1884. It was to be the gift of the Duke of Norfolk to his fellow Catholics of Norwich. The first Mass was sung in the nave in 1894, and the complete church was opened in 1910. The wheel had turned full circle in little more than four hundred years.

CHAPTER FIVE

Norwich Cathedral — A Great Benedictine Priory Church

O F ALL English cathedrals that of Norwich is historically and architecturally one of the most satisfying to study. It has miraculously survived in a way that presents to the twentieth century its dual features of monastic church and cathedral of the diocese. All the more remarkable this when we recall the centuries of dissension that soured relations between the great Benedictine monastery and the citizens of the city surrounding its precincts.

The history of those quarrels and of many another like them masks the truth regarding the irreparable loss to the country and the community created by Henry VIII when he ordered the wholesale Dissolution of the Monasteries in 1535-36. In this generation the effect would be similar were every amenity of the Welfare State suddenly to be withdrawn. Though the monastic system had its faults it had given much towards man's progress. It had provided an education whereby a poor boy might rise to the highest office in the land. It gave relief to the poor and suffering, medicine, doctors and hospitals for the sick and the old. Not until after the Reformation was there need for Poor Laws and Vagrancy Acts. It ensured hospitality for the wayfarer and maintained safeguards and guidance both on sea and land. Trinity House is one of our legacies from this work. In agriculture the monasteries did more than teach progress, they made it. Before the age of printing they were the only places where books were available, for monks formed the majority of copyists of existing books. (In important houses such as Norwich fair copies of the rolls were written by specially engaged scriveners or clerks.) Indeed it was the monasteries which steered Europe out of the Dark Ages. When in the course of time mediaeval thought gave way to that of the Renaissance it was the monastic libraries to which students came to unearth the pearls of Classical thought long enshrined in them.

Norwich Cathedral is a memorial both to the virtues of the mediaeval church and to the faith of its builders and those who have preserved it for us. The hand of the desecrator was never so heavy on its fabric as to wipe clean its original purpose nor the zeal of the restorer rabid enough to blot out the pristine purity of its architecture. The result is a Benedictine church mainly Romanesque in style, built by Saxon workmen, sculptors and carpenters alike, under the direction of perhaps a few Norman masons all carrying out the expressed wishes of the founder, Bishop Herbert de Losinga.

Norwich Cathedral: the north presbytery aisle with its unique feature, a reliquary arch.

Norwich Cathedral: apsidal east end showing the successful welding of Gothic with the Romanesque.

The foundations under St Saviour's Chapel are as first set out by the Normans. They seem quickly to have changed their scheme to a longer apsidal chapel. There is no evidence of shoddy work at Norwich. In 1964 it was discovered that the foundations of the great tower were six feet deep and built on a solid gravel stratum.

Bishop Losinga undoubtedly was given a clear site. There had been a church of the Holy Trinity; it is mentioned in Domesday Book and was possibly under the north transept; it was not monastic but a private-cum-parochial church. In fact the whole of the monastic area now known as the Close, apart from the water meadows, had been a section of the Saxon town abutting on the central market known as Tombland till after 1066.

Herbert de Losinga was a Benedictine. He naturally set great store upon processional activities as part of the future ritual. So he and his master masons adopted the ambulatory plan for his church. This entailed a processional walk carried right round the perimeter and to the east of the high altar. The twentieth century visitor as he follows aisle and ambulatory will realise that he thus circumnavigates the cathedral. This detail of Benedictine practice remains more clearly defined in Norwich than in any other English cathedral.

An ambulatory plan around the outside of the great presbytery apse allowed the development of apsidiole chapels to the North-east, East and South-east. The first and third remain. The eastern chapel disappeared when the former Lady Chapel was built on its site in the thirteenth century. However, the apsidiole chapels and the presbytery were ready for consecration by 1101. Before Losinga's death in 1119 he had probably completed the transepts, the lower part of the central tower and four bays of the nave. It seems certain that the nave was completed by his successor, Eborard, before 1145. In 1171 a fire occurred but it is hard to say what damage was done. Far worse was the great fire of 1272 brought about by a conflict between the citizens and the monastery. Though faults existed on both sides Henry III imposed heavy fines on the city that went towards the building of the Ethelbert Gateway into the monastic precincts (today known as the Close) replacing a church to the S. E. of the site that had suffered destruction during the riots. The remainder of the fine helped repair the cathedral.

In 1362 a great gale from the west blew down the spire. Whether the spire was of wood is not clear but highly probable. It collapsed onto the presbytery, ruined the clerestory which was rebuilt on a grand High Gothic scale about 1330. Chapels were erected on north and south sides of the presbytery, some windows inserted in the west wall of the north transept and a doorway opened on the north side of the nave.

In the fifteenth century disaster again overtook the cathedral, another great fire in 1463. The wooden roof of the nave came crashing down, crushing the

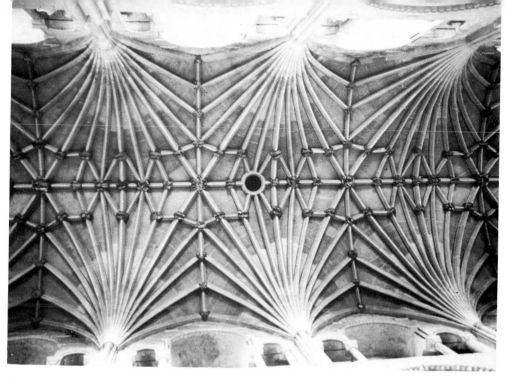

Norwich Cathedral nave: the lierne vaulting by Bishop Lyhart.

Norwich Cathedral: Bishop Lyhart's rebus above the nave arcade.

Norman bases of the piers: which is why they today all have Perpendicular bases. This brought home to Bishop Lyhart, the Prior and the Chapter the crying need for stone vaulting which till then had only been used for aisles and apses. The Bishop made himself responsible for the new and lovely lierne vaulting of the nave. You can see his rebus, a hart lying in water, between every third and fourth arch of the gallery, on a corbel carrying a vaulting shaft. A rebus is a pun on a man's name, executed in stone or wood. Bearing in mind that names such as Walpole and Walter were pronounced Worpole and Water in Norfolk the force of 'Walter Ly hart' becomes clear.

Twenty years later his successor, Bishop Goldwell vaulted the presbytery but it needed another fire in 1509 before the transepts received their vaults. The ancient wooden roof of the presbytery, above the vaulting, was not removed until 1955.

These, then, are the chief mediaeval vicissitudes which have afflicted the cathedral and which have paradoxically added enormously not only to the glory of the fabric but to its interest as well. Some account now follows of the cathedral's chief features. As in my experience, the majority of visitors enter the north aisle by its west door we will begin our itinerary and detailed description there.

The Nave

Stand on the steps at the west end and look along the nave and up at the vaulted roof. Let the grandeur of the whole project soak into you and marvel at the skill, the inspiration, the adventure of it all. You will feel overwhelmed, unable to give your attention to detail. Yet slowly you realise that you are seeing the combination of musical Romanesque arcades, galleries and clerestories with the perfection of Late Gothic vaulting. Of course, such perfection can only arise when the master masons are both artists and architects. That in these days many architects are not artists stands out a mile.

Next you realise that you are looking down three corridors, the nave and its two aisles, the nave terminating at Lyhart's stone pulpitum on which stands the organ. This is not the actual end of the nave for the Benedictine rule carried the choir two bays westward. The cathedral nave is the only one in England of fourteen bays. The four eastern arches are the work of the founder, the remainder that of his successor who ceased to be Bishop of Norwich in 1145. Most of the piers are shafted, but, mysteriously enough, two are massive round columns with spiral channelling. Further east on the north side was a similar column but, for reasons unknown there was a mind change and this too became shafted.* Glance up at the gallery above. This is as massive as the arcading and similar both in style and height. Above is the clerestory. Here it is possible to see how cleverly the

*Latest theory regarding the cylindrical pillars with spiral decoration is that there were originally four, their purpose being to frame the original nave sanctuary where today the nave altar stands. The spiral decoration shows Byzantine influence.

Norwich Cathedral: the crossing and nave vaulting.

Norwich Cathedral nave: showing the skilful wedding of Romanesque with thirteenth century lierne vaulting.

great cones of lierne vaulting have been wedded to the Romanesque. Now move down the nave and look back to the west. The great Late Gothic window was put in by Bishop Alnwick's executors but the west front was altered by Bishop Alnwick himself and is, in comparison with the rest of the fabric, a rather tame affair. The glass is nineteenth century, by Helgeland, a memorial to Bishop Stanley.

Inevitably, over the centuries, while the basic design has remained unchanged, details, such as the west front, become remodelled. Lyhart's pulpitum is another example of this. The archway leading to the choir is practically all that is left of his work. In 1833 Salvin, a ruthless restorer, remade the coving and later, to be in keeping with his lovely new organ case, Stephen Dykes-Bower redesigned the Gothic parapet in 1950.

The organ is the sixth since the twelfth century, fires or riots having destroyed the previous five. Indeed, the Reformation brought no end to troublesome times. Norfolk, having economic links with the Low Countries became early a stronghold of extreme Protestant thought and there were four eruptions of iconoclasm between 1536 and the outbreak of Civil War in 1649. The Cathedral lost its organ, brasses, monuments, stained glass, ornaments, vestments and a library of mediaeval missals and breviaries. Fortunately its wonderful collection of monastic records (1250 yards of parchment) were not thought sufficiently papistical for destruction.

Most sad is the picture of desecration which must have occurred early after the Reformation. The words of Matthew Parker, Elizabeth's archbishop of Canterbury give the clearest possible description. "The choir is an utter desolation. It had long ago been cleared of everything valuable, ornaments, service books, lamps, vestments and tapestries. The pictured glass of the windows was broken, the font thrown down." The final ignominy came a hundred years later when Great Yarmouth petitioned Cromwell to allow them to use the stone of that "useless old cathedral in Norwich" to build a workhouse and repair the harbour works.

Let us continue our walk. On the south side of the nave the first tomb chest is that of Chancellor Spencer, last Dean of the College of St Mary in the Field. The college stood on the site of the present Norwich Assembly Rooms and in pre-Reformation days was probably the wealthiest college of priests in the country. Next is Bishop Nikke's chantry chapel (1501-1536). The Norman arches above have been changed to four centred arches and are rich with colourful Tudor heraldry. The next tomb eastward is that of Bishop Parkhurst (1560-1575).

There are two tomb chests on the north side. The first is that of Sir Thomas Windham, Privy Councillor, member of Henry VIII's bodyguard and a vice admiral. The other tomb chest is Sir James Hobart's. He was Attorney General to Henry VII, lived at Hales Court and built Loddon church.

Before leaving the nave mention must be made of the roof bosses, those sculptured pictures mediaeval masons put at the intersections of the vaulting ribs. The great height of these above the floor makes any prolonged study of them a neck-breaking task. Covering as they do the "people's church" as distinct from the monastic church east of the pulpitum, they might be described as the "picture book" of mediaeval man. More will be said on this subject in the chapter on Church Imagery. For the moment a brief description is necessary to bring coherence into this galaxy of bosses, some 225 in all.

In the first seven bays from the east they illustrate the Old Testament, and New Testament scenes are depicted in the remaining seven bays. The Old Testament portion begins with the Creation and ends with the accession of Solomon. This was not uncommonly the terminus chosen by mediaeval artists who found it difficult to portray the Prophets and the Epistles. As you will find later in the cloisters it is easier to mark the place in the story with the large central bosses of the bays. In Bay I east of the crossing are scenes from the Creation, the Fall, the legendary death of Cain — shot by blind Lamech with an arrow. Bay II gives the story of Noah and the Flood. Bay III has the Tower of Babel, the sacrifice of Isaac and the deceit of Jacob. At this point order becomes haphazard and bosses belonging to adjacent bays become interchanged. Bay IV tells the story of Jacob, the ladder, the peeling of the rods, the wrestling with an angel. Bay V contains the story of Joseph and linking up with Bay VI, Joseph and his brethren. Bay VI contains Moses at the burning bush and the crossing of the Red Sea. Bay VII has the gates of Gaza and Samson shorn by Delilah; then David and Goliath, David and Solomon and the anointing of the last mentioned. Bay VIII begins with Solomon enthroned.

The New Testament stories follow the usual course beginning with the Annunciation. The Nativity, Adoration of the Magi and Massacre of the Innocents follow. Bay IX has the Flight into Egypt, Christ and the Doctors, the Baptism, Cana, the Temptation, the Raising of Lazarus. Bay X the entry into Jerusalem, the Last Supper and Washing of the Feet. Bay XI the Betrayal, Trial and Mockery, Bay XII the Crucifixion, Burial and Harrowing in Hell, and Bay XIII the Resurrection, Appearances, Ascension and Pentecost. Bay XIV is devoted to the Last Judgement and at the extreme west Bishop Lyhart himself is represented.

We move forward into the transepts. The north appears severe but it contains some of the earliest and least spoiled work in the cathedral. Note particularly the "beaked" or headed window arches in the north wall, a typically Saxon feature. Below is a plain Norman door with no tympanum, traditionally the Bishop's door, his private entrance to the cathedral. A Norman arch in the east wall is the entrance to St Andrew's chapel, apsidal, and part of the original *chevet* plan of the Benedictine church. It has a three-light Early English window containing glass originally in the Deanery where Cardinal Wolsey stayed in 1524 when settling disputes here. Just to the right of the chapel is a Norman arch with tympanum filled with a diaper design, one of only two in the county.

The south transept, by contrast has suffered considerable change during the centuries. Its southern portion was formerly the cathedral gaol. The two Jacobean quarter jacks are all that remains of a mediaeval clock destroyed in the seventeenth century. It would have been one of those mediaeval clocks that in their time ranked among the marvels of technical achievement. The Sacrist's rolls of 1322-25 give details of moneys spent on fifty-nine images, robes, glue, gold leaf, paint and cymbals needed in its construction.

Both transepts were given their vaults by Bishop Nikke after the fire of 1509. The bosses on these continue and at times duplicate Lyhart's New Testament series with subjects from the life of Christ and of the Virgin, with Old Testament incidents interspersed. For example the Flight into Egypt occurs eight times and the angel appears to Joseph nine times.

The appearance of the south transept is spoiled by Salvin's attempt to recreate a Norman arcade around it. Otherwise it is one of the finest examples of early Norman work in existence. It has lost the corresponding apsidiole chapel, the site now being occupied by Chapter offices.

The Presbytery Aisles And Ambulatory

We come now to the north presbytery aisle, enclosed from the transepts by screens, the northern one being a copy of that in the south ambulatory, which was the work of Robert Catton, one of the last Priors (1520-1529). His initials are on the lock. The blank wall arcading, so characteristic a feature of Norman walling, is again apparent here as in the nave aisles. Immediately facing us is a structure known as the "Reliquary Arch", a unique feature. The two vaulted bays were built in 1278 and it was extended about three feet east and west in 1424. North of this was a reliquary chapel built in 1398 and it seems that the arch was for the purpose of displaying relics at a safe distance above pilgrims' heads. Its liturgical importance is evidenced by the richness of the mural paintings above, dating from the early fourteenth century and depicting Christ together with saints and apostles. This relic chamber has again become a place for the display of historic treasures for, through the munificence of the Worshipful Company of Goldsmiths of London it was, in 1972, arranged as a treasury for the exhibiting of plate hitherto unused and unseen, from parishes in the diocese.

East of the bridge we are in the semicircular ambulatory around the sanctuary, a singularly fine piece of Saxo-Norman work, and on the left is the north-east apsidiole Jesus chapel, part of the original *chevet*. Like St Luke's chapel on the south-east, its shape is unusual. Instead of projecting straight out as is usual with

Norwich Cathedral: the Jesus chapel, part of the original chevet plan. Beneath the altar cloth is the stone mensa.

eastern chapels these are constructed in two parts. In each case the apse is turned to face due east, while a horseshoe shape ante-chapel connects it with the ambulatory. Dean Thurlow of Gloucester considers this emphasis on facing the altars east may have been due to the force of our pagan traditions. "Sun worship still meant more to us than to the Europeans!" he cogently remarks. The apse is vaulted with the usual semi-dome vault. Recent restoration has ensured that the wall painting has been carefully cleaned, recovering as far as possible its thirteenth century appearance as well as that of the Norman work still existing.

The Jesus chapel contains an unusual feature, a mediaeval stone altar slab, or mensa, of the twelfth century. The holes on the north, east and south sides probably show that a reredos was fixed to it. Extremely rare is the 'seal' of the altar, a square slab of Purbeck marble, probably later in date, measuring 22½ inches by 20¼ inches and marked with the usual five crosses. It covers a shallow recess in the altar for minute fragments of holy relics.

Before continuing further, cross over to the sanctuary and glance up at the springing of the gallery arch opposite. Take note of the Norman face gazing proudly at you, the aquiline nose, the moustache, the insolent eyes. From a similar position on the south-east, you will be able to see its counterpart, a caricature of a Saxon head, loutish, pimply and diffused. They tell the old legend of the building of the cathedral, how that Losinga, in a hurry, employed both Saxon and Norman workmen. The latter, being the master race, built the south side, the Saxons the north. To show this they each put up their heads as seal to their work and for ever the conqueror gazes disdainfully at his vanquished foe.

Norwich Cathedral: Norman arrogance above the south presbytery.

Norwich Cathedral: caricature of the Saxon face above the north presbytery.

Norwich Cathedral: early fourteenth century entrance to the Lady chapel — now St Saviour's chapel and War Memorial.

Resuming our tour we reach St Saviour's Chapel. It is the fourth place of worship on this site. Its first must have had some association with the Saxon west wall of the cloisters, the date probably 1091-6, forming part of Losinga's first building before a Norman mason was available. His second chapel on the site was an apsidiole which was demolished by Bishop Suffield (1245-57) who built a much larger rectangular Lady Chapel. This, a wonderful example of Early English Gothic, was let fall into ruin in the sixteenth century. All that remains today are ruins of the walls outside; within are two elegant entrance arches rich with deep mouldings and dogtooth ornament and above, a quatrefoil. Pillars and responds supporting these arches were replaced in Perpendicular style following fire damage in 1463. After the Reformation the space of the chapel was occupied by a house and garden for many years and the arches blocked up. In 1930 the present chapel of St Saviour was begun and consecrated in 1932 as a war memorial to those who died in the First World War and as a thanksgiving for the cathedral's preservation. It was designed by Sir Charles Nicholson and the iron screen, designed by Stephen Dykes Bower, was made by Eric Stevenson of Wroxham. The window glass represents the four East Anglian saints, Edmund, Julian, Fursey and Felix. The fine mediaeval panels came originally from the church of St Michael at Plea in nearby Queen Street.

In the south ambulatory St Luke's Chapel, apsidiole with a horseshoe ante chapel, similar to the Jesus Chapel already described, completes all that is left of the Benedictine *chevet*. It too contains considerable traces of early painting. Indeed both chapels go far to make the visitor realise what a colourful place was a great mediaeval monastic church. Ecclesiastically the chapel occupies a peculiar if not unique position. An ancient parish church, that of St Mary in the Marsh, standing within the cathedral precincts, was demolished in the reign of Elizabeth I and the Cathedral Chapter allowed the parishioners to have use of the chapel. The living is in the gift of the Dean and Chapter. The font at the entrance, one of Norfolk's many seven sacrament fonts, but a sadly damaged one, was brought from the old church. Rubrics in the thirteenth century Customary indicate a font near the west end of the nave, otherwise there seems never to have been a baptistery.

In a shallow recess beside the chapel is a remarkable effigy, long thought to be that of the founder, Herbert de Losinga. Until 1967 it occupied a niche above the Bishops' doorway in the north transept where, on removal, it was found to have been built in. This gives the lie to its once having been Losinga's tomb or coffin lid. That it is not an effigy of himself is obvious; he would never have countenanced any reproduction of himself being set up in the Cathedral. More-over the stone is ancient. Mr Feilden, the cathedral architect, has established that it has some affinity with box-ground Bath stone and this could indicate a pre-Conquest date. So it could be contemporary with the Bishop's cathedral that most certainly came from North Elmham and probably was moved there from

Norwich Cathedral: the effigy long thought to be that of Losinga but now considered to be Pope Gregory.

Dummoc, leaving us with the possibility that the effigy is that of Pope Gregory. Though the head is uncrowned and unmitred the vestments seem to point towards this supposition, the left hand holds a pastoral staff which has mostly survived, its head visible near his ear and his right hand is raised in benediction. The figure is flanked with spiral shafts on lion head bases. Here the question of identity must rest.

It should be noted that both the Jesus and St Luke's chapels are vaulted to carry above each another chamber. That above the Jesus chapel is the Cathedral museum. Above the St Luke's chapel is the Muniment Chamber where are housed charters and Obedientary Rolls.

The retable behind the altar is work by Norwich artists of about 1381. It was given by Norfolk nobles and by Bishop Le Despenser to commemorate the defeat of John Litester, local leader of the Peasants' Revolt. At the Reformation it was saved by being turned over and used as a table top. Not until 1847 was the ruse discovered and the restored retable returned to the cathedral. In the south window is a good specimen of fifteenth century Norwich glass depicting the Virgin and Child. The other windows are Victorian.

Continuing our walk westwards, on our left is the Bauchon chapel built early in the fourteenth century by William Bauchon, Granarius of the monastery. The walls were raised and the roof vaulted a hundred years later. The vault is in two bays, the central boss of the south bay depicting the Assumption of the Blessed Virgin and that of the north bay her Coronation. The rest tell a story familiar in the Middle Ages and retold by Chaucer in the Man of Laws Tale. The chapel, once used as the Consistory Court has been restored and renamed "The Chapel of the Friends of Norwich Cathedral." The fenestration, Victorian Gothic, is filled with glass by Miss Moira Forsyth and depicts the great Benedictine figures of history. Within a niche, a lovely piece of fifteenth century work, stands the modern figure of Our Lady of Pity. The entrance screen of wrought iron was designed by Mr Bernard Feilden, the Cathedral architect and made by Mr Eric Stevenson of Wroxham.

Farther to the west we pass the door to the Chapter Room. On its walls hang portraits of early Deans, including William Castleton, the last Prior, who, on the conversion of the Priory, became the first Dean (1538). The Renaissance oak panelling on the east and west walls is said to have come from St Benet's Abbey on the River Bure. Association between the cathedral and St Benet's Abbey is unusual. At the Dissolution the Bishop's revenue was found to be more valuable than that of St Benet's Abbot. The latter Henry VIII considered sufficient for a bishop. So the very convenient transfer was made. The consequence of this is that today the Bishop of Norwich, as titular Abbot of St Benet's, is the only mitred abbot in the established church.

Norwich Cathedral, St Luke's chapel. The fourteenth century retable.

Having reached the end of the presbytery south aisle we shall turn into the presbytery. But before we do, let us go and stand beneath the great Norman lantern, or tower, the finest in England. About at level with the presbytery roof seems to be the summit of Losinga's work and the tower was eventually finished by Bishop Turbe. Above it rises the spire, the fourth on the site. The first, presumably a low one of the Rhenish type was burnt in the riot of 1272. By 1297 Peter Koc had built another of wood sheathed in lead. This blew down on to the presbytery in 1362. The third, again of timber, was struck by lightning in 1463 when much of the main roofing was burned necessitating the vaulting of the nave and the present spire was built by Bishop Goldwell in 1480.

The tower contains five bells, historically of great interest but campano-logically the worst in any English cathedral. They were cast by the Brasyer family who maintained the Norwich bell foundry in the fifteenth century. Since 1751 they have hung 'dead' and can only be chimed, but their sweet minor tones have a peculiarly peaceful, rural quality as they speak out the quarters over the Cathedral Close throughout the daylight hours.

The Presbytery

The most important feature in the Cathedral, historically and ecclesiastically, is the Bishop's Throne raised high beneath the most easterly arch of the presbytery apse. Fundamentally what is left of the original beneath its crimson covering could be of any date between A.D. 600 and A.D. 1000. Of a certainty it formed part of the Bishop's Throne in North Elmham Cathedral, but could it have come first from Dummoc? That it has been venerated from earliest times is certain or why should Losinga have worried to bring those two pieces of carved but battered stone from the old to be set up in his new cathedral?

The two pieces are arms, that to the south a clear support. The north piece is probably the north west terminal of a semi-circle too large for the North Elmham apse, an indication that it could have come from Dummoc. The North Elmham apse has a projecting respond that would have hidden a carved arm.

In the eighth century it was customary for a throne to form part of a semi-circle of seats called a *synthronos* around the apse. The practice died out in the twelfth century but the throne remained, now to be the only Bishop's Throne in such a position north of the Alps. As in St Peter's, Rome a shaft beneath the Bishop's feet communicates with a reliquary below, the lower outlet of which may be seen from the ambulatory.

Despite restoration the apse remains the least altered of that of any other cathedral in England. Losinga's haste to get the work done is evident here in the simple, unornamented style of pillars and capitals. Originally the sides of the presbytery must have carried on with the general plan but after the collapse of the spire in 1362 Bishop Thomas Percy rebuilt the clerestory in a manner truly magnificent and Bishop Goldwell remodelled the arcade in 1495 and erected the vault above the clerestory. Faint traces of colouring on the walls reveal what was probably a general scheme of decoration put in hand after the fire of 1272.

Few monuments of interest remain in the Cathedral, owing in part to the destruction of 1643. In the centre of the presbytery is a slate ledger slab commemorating the founder Bishop Losinga. The Cathedral's finest chantry chapel is on the south side of the presbytery. It is that of Bishop Goldwell (1499). His effigy, retaining the mediaeval colouring, is vested in albe, stole, tunica, dalmatic, cope, mitre, gloves and staff. The chantry is heavily canopied with tracery, finials and crockets and with pendants below. The sympathetic colouring of the canopy was added by Professor Tristram just before the war. Bishop Goldwell's rebus, a gold well-top, can be seen on many of the presbytery bosses.

The sanctuary furnishings are modern. The altar, designed by Sir Charles Nicholson was erected in 1933 and its candlesticks were given by the Corporation in 1665 replacing those destroyed during the Commonwealth. The mosaic floor and the communion rails of bronze and spars were designed in 1878 by Sir A. W. Blomefield and given by Dean Goulburn.

It will be noticed that the Benedictine practice of the choir being in the nave, is found here at Norwich, as at Westminster and elsewhere. It takes up the two eastern bays and contains one of the finest examples of choir stalls and canopies in England. They were first erected in 1420 but when many of them were destroyed in the fire of 1463 the survivors were rearranged. These are the sixteen westernmost canopies each side. More had been added to these in 1480 by Bishop Goldwell. All now occupy the same position as the Norman ones burnt in 1272. In several places, instead of the leaf crocket, the hawk, symbol of Bishop Wakering (1416-25) is displayed. Shields beneath the misericords — so named because by this 'merciful' dispensation monks could rest against them while 'standing' for long periods of the services — indicate the families whose members gave towards their erection. The imagery beneath the misericords will be discussed later in the chapter on Imagery and Furnishings. The device of the lectern, dating from the fourteenth century, depicts the pelican in her piety, feeding her young on drops of her blood. She is shown pecking at her breast. The nest containing the young unfortunately disappeared long ago.

The Cloister

Here is the largest monastic cloister in England, larger than Westminster, larger than Durham. The plan prepared by Mr Whittingham, Archaeological Consultant to the Dean and Chapter, shows that in most respects the great

The Saxon Bishop's throne.

monastery at Norwich followed the generally accepted Benedictine plan. Most of the monastic buildings lay to the south of the church and were grouped around the cloisters.

Cloisters have always served several purposes, as a living room in which to sit for a period each day in silence, for processions, for the daily washing of faces and hands and for the ceremonial washing of feet. Near by in cubicles were tubs of hot water for shaving and for bathing at intervals of perhaps six weeks. The cloisters connected under cover the various monastic buildings. They were used as a parliamentary forum for the airing of practical problems and in some monasteries as a *scriptorium* for the monks. (It is doubtful if this last purpose ever prevailed at Norwich for the fenestration, other than just the tracery above, has never been glazed.) So, the cloister served more than just a protection from inclement weather but acted as a communal bond, an emphasis laid upon all Benedictine houses by the Founder himself. It is possible that the upper storeys, a feature unique to Norwich, acted as the *scriptorium* — those on the east, west and south sides being still used.

There is some doubt whether the upper storey on the north side was ever roofed.

These are not the first cloisters. Before the twelfth century was out there were Norman cloisters of stone but after the fire of 1272 rebuilding took place and the work was done over a period of 150 years. This accounts for changes in the fenestration tracery though the design of pillars, buttresses, arches and vaults remains constant. Of Norman work is the east cloister wall and even earlier the west wall for it contains evidence, in the splayed round windows, of Saxon workmanship.

The stone roof is a fine example of intermediate rib vaulting with over 400 carved bosses. One of the earliest rebuilt features is the lovely doorway leading into the south aisle of the nave and wrongly called the Prior's Door. It was in practice the main doorway to the church, used by the monks many times in the course of each twenty-four hours. Radiating across the arch are seven figures each canopied. In the centre Christ, flanked by angels, sits in judgment, displaying his wounds. Farther left is St Edmund and Moses and right, St Peter and John the Baptist. The detached shafts, with heavy roll moulding caps and bases, are of Purbeck marble.

Both doors were used for the great Sunday processions which took place after High Mass. The monks left their places in the choir, sprinkled all altars with holy water and went around the cloister. Continuing up the nave they made a solemn station before the screen which was one bay west of the *pulpitum,* passing through the two doors of the screen, converged to the one door of the *pulpitum* and so back to their stalls.

Norwich Cathedral: early fourteenth century ceremonial entrance from the cloisters. Note the detached pillars. Figures above are of Christ in glory flanked with angels and the three saints Peter, Edmund, John the Baptist and the patriarch Moses.

Norwich Cathedral: early fourteenth century book cupboards in the east wall of the cloisters.

As one leaves the church for the east walk some book cupboards are apparent, three canopied arches, two of which are blocked. In the east and south walks are other cupboards, explanation of which has not been found. The fine fourteenth century arch blocked in the east wall led to the slype or passage to the cemetery and the parlour where monks were allowed a measure of conversation. The three open arches once led to the Chapter House. Beyond it on the south side was the common room, where in winter monks had a fire. Over these buildings was the dormitory the entrance to which still remains. It is the thirteenth century arch south of the Chapter house. The step at the entrance on its south side still shows wear from the passage of the monks' sandalled feet.

Farther south again is finely moulded thirteenth century arch through which the Prior went to his Lodge, now the Deanery. At the end of the east walk is the Dark Entry. It led to the Infirmary, a fine aisled hall of the twelfth century of which only a few pillars remain. Here lived permanently the old monks. Any who were sick were admitted during their illness and monks were allowed to go there for three days after bleeding, for warmth and better food.

Along the south side was the great *refectorium,* or frater, the dining hall of the monks. Though ruined it retains the north and much of the south and east, but the pulpit and the raised dais for the high table have disappeared. The kitchens were at the west end.

In the south west corner is the *lavatorium.* It takes up two bays. Means whereby water was fed to the spot have long disappeared but the stone trough which received the waste water still remains. Farther north a doorway, similar in moulding to that of the frater, was the monks' entrance to the guest house. The guests' entrance still remains to the north west of it, a lovely archway of late thirteenth century.

The western range of monastic buildings is all gone except the northern part which is now used as the Cathedral shop. It was once the parlour where the monks were allowed to meet their friends. Much of it dates from the twelfth century but it was enlarged at the west and a new doorway made at the east in the thirteenth century.

In mediaeval times the cloister garth was never used for burials. All the present graves are modern and include those of Bishop Sheepshanks, Deans Willink and Cranage and Canon Hay Aitken.

CHAPTER SIX

Church Imagery

T O UNDERSTAND the iconography of the mediaeval church, of which today only vestiges remain, one has to delve not only into the dark recesses of man's mind but into the even darker pages of his past. Imagery is as old as mankind's earliest religious yearnings. It primarily represents a longing to make manifest those deep-seated fears, mysteries and aspirations which have always accompanied man's awakening reason and, by making them manifest, cushion their impact on his mind and his spirit. The crude fertility goddess figure found in the Stone Age flint workings known as Grimes Graves at Weeting, the beak heads above Saxon arches, the Pope Gregory above Haddiscoe south door, the numerous St Christophers painted on north walls facing the door, the screens, the roods, the bench ends, and the statuary of the mediaeval church all possess the same fundamental significance, they assuage the mind, they help interpret the unknown, they help guide man's erring steps.

The later influence of a priestly caste introduced another important factor, that of secret knowledge. The priest became the repository and interpreter of this knowledge and, as time passed, tended to act as a filter, allowing only that to be displayed to the ignorant which a hierarchical priesthood considered safe for them to know. The last and most advanced step was when the priest became the imparter rather than the interpreter of knowledge.

Mediaeval churches were primarily places of worship made as attractive and beautiful as the skill and resources of their builders would allow, to the greater glory of God and sometimes to enhance the status of men. But when it comes to the imagery contained within and without the church, then the underlying purpose was to express in the simplest way the teaching of the Church to all who entered and particularly the great multitude of those who could not read. So we can say that the figures in stained glass, the wall paintings and carvings were all pages from the Picture Book of the Unlearned. What remains of it today has an increased value for us if we understand sufficient about its composition to be able to interpret what we see.

The principles were fundamentally simple because they all to some extent conformed to a master plan. The French archaeologist, Didron, discovered an ancient Manual for Painters in use in Mount Athos monastery in 1839, tradition of which dated back to the seventh century. It specified Old and New Testament subjects and gave positions appropriate to each on the walls. The painted murals of some early churches as, for instance, Shelfanger All Saints, Potter Heigham and Wickhampton St Andrew illustrate a few of the principles underlying the placing of much mediaeval imagery. It was later that gilds and chantries disrupted this ancient over-all planning with their own imagery.

The mediaeval church used every resource to stress moral contrasts; Doom and Redemption, Good and Evil were shown in dramatic opposition to highlight the gulf that lay between the haven of Holy Church and the rocks and whirlpools existing outside it. Teaching began at the church door, was overpoweringly emphasised by the Doom over the chancel arch and underlined by the Ascension and Christ seated in Glory above the altar. The series of bosses on the chancel roof of SS Peter and Paul at Salle present the life of Christ from the Annunciation to the Ascension.

Iconographical significance of the church door lost ground with later church builders, perhaps because a porch came to be built, secular use of which obscured its liturgical importance. The figure of Pope Gregory above the south door of Haddiscoe St Mary indicates that the Saxons fully realised the symbolic impact of the door. The present obscurity of this sculpture reveals its later loss of importance. Elsewhere in the country such symbolism occurs on Saxo-Norman tympanums but Norfolk has no examples of these.

Mediaeval imagery was not squeamish. Relics of pagan worship were neither ridiculed nor despised. One might go so far as to say that the remarkable respect shown to the Devil and his myrmidons could be evidence of this. Additionally, the green man — Pan — peeping through leafage appears on many a sculptured boss in the vaulting of Norwich Cathedral cloisters. At the same time, disposition of subjects in nave and chancel, on walls and roofs, could make the humblest village church portray the entire Universe of Space and the ultimate limits of Time. The roof represented the heavens so all its glories came to be painted upon it. Necton All Saints has wonderful colour decoration; figures stand upon wall posts, angels with outspread wings hang upon the hammer beams and a deep cornice carries two rows of angels between the brattishing, the purlins being adorned with flowers at all intersections. Knapton roof is literally a-flutter with angels, Cawston St Agnes has figures standing on the hammer beams at the foot of the arch braces.

If it is at all possible today to determine from the remaining vestiges a scheme of imagery purely British, then it would seem that the nave was devoted to instruction of the laity. Windows and mural decoration illustrated the earthly lives of Christ and of his saints and included amid them the previously mentioned moral allegories. At Potter Heigham St Nicholas is probably the earliest example of the Works of Mercy. At Weston Longville is the Tree of Jesse hung with figures executed in simple earth colours. At Sporle St Mary are twenty-four scenes from the life of St Catherine of Alexandria coloured green, red, yellow ochre and black. At Edingthorpe All Saints a fragment of the Works of Mercy hangs from the branches of trees. Witching and jangling (idle talk) are recorded as once being on the walls of Colton St Andrew, Little Melton St Mary, Seething St Margaret and Stokesby St Andrew. At Fring All Saints a large St Christopher is on the north wall, a piece of a scroll above the chancel arch and a saint in a red tunic on the south wall. At West Somerton St Mary are faint vestiges of the Entry into Jerusalem, the Scourging and the Resurrection on the north wall and a Last Judgment with a St Christopher on the south wall. But vestiges of the Last Judgment and Doom are rare in Norfolk because the theme was frequently extended to the north-east and south-east aisle windows. We find at Martham St Mary the South-east window illustrates the Weighing of Souls by St Michael, a common piece of Doom iconography. The impact of the Doom later added significance to the great cross of the rood loft framed within the arch.

Mediaeval imagery had two advantages. However poorly executed, its basic symbols were easily recognisable by a public which ranged from a highly educated clergy to the illiterate peasant. The stories could be interpreted historically, typologically or sacramentally. It is just this remarkable flexibility which deters us today from rejecting as naive the whole picture book scheme. The ubiquitous St Christophers directly incited the ignorant towards gentleness and a rejection of brutality. The less ignorant saw in the message the promise that "whoso looked upon the image, that day should not die an ill death" — that is a death without the rites of the church. So, St Christophers always faced the most used door of the church.

In Norfolk churches whose foundation can be dated earlier than the twelfth century, mural paintings appear to have been frequently carried out in sepia and of this sufficient evidence remains to suggest a once complete covering of the walls with colour. In 1857 following the removal of many coats of whitewash at Catfield All Saints and Crostwight St Peter a wide distribution of paintings of the north walls was uncovered. Unique in Norfolk was the Tree of Seven Deadly Sins. This iconography is a milder form than that which inspired Lydgate to write:

> Many wonderful ymages
> Ful ougly of ther visages
> Methought yt dyde ne gret good
> To beholde the purtreytures.

In Crostwight the work included a giant St Christopher and an Annunciation and Crucifixion as well as vestiges of a number of other subjects, one group seated around a table over which hovers a demon.

It is impossible to say whether the impact of these murals decreased with time but it is significant that later alterations to the fabric often cut drastically

Catfield All Saints. Tree of the Seven Deadly Sins.

into many a picture. At Hemblington a wall post destroyed some of the upper strip pictures detailing St Christopher's life and at Potter Heigham one entirely obliterates part of a Seven Mercies series. At St George Colegate, Norwich, a fifteenth century window has wiped out all but the fringe of a thirteenth century painting. This surely points to their having become obsolete. While imagery as a means of teaching moral and spiritual values remained until the Reformation and after, methods could have changed with the centuries. By the late fourteenth and well into the sixteenth century the medium had shifted to the painted screen and the rood, together with stained glass, carved bench ends and arm rests. So it is a possibility that walls were already being whitewashed in order to hide the old pictures. I think it probable that, had they still been widely exposed at the time of the Reformation and after they would have been defaced instead of being only covered up. Few murals appear to have suffered deliberate defacement other than those depicting the Martyrdom of Becket. Happily the whitewash of centuries has saved these vestiges for us. The majority have been lost by exposure followed by neglect and indifference.

In other respects too, changes of iconography are reasonably easy to detect. Scandinavian, or Viking subjects are absent from Norfolk but for fragments, an interlaced wheel cross at Whissonsett St Mary, another at Ringstead St Andrew and the remains of a sandstone cross shaft from the now non-existent church of St Vedast, Norwich. In the tenth century the Martyrdom of Kings became a popular theme that failed to seize strongly the East Anglian imagination. There are however nine dedications in Norfolk to St Edmund, King of the East Angles who was slaughtered by the Danes in A.D. 870, probably after a battle fought at Hellesdon near Norwich. His emblems, a hand grasping arrows, appears occasionally

Crostwight All Saints. Paintings on the north wall. Over the door a devil at the feast and below a St Christopher.

View of the North Wall of Crostwight Church, Norfolk.
1847.

and his birth and martyrdom are represented on cloister bosses in Norwich Cathedral. The story that his head was recovered by a wolf appears on a bench end at Walpole St Peter and on the stone parapet of Pulham St Mary. Screen panels at Barnham Broom, Barton Turf and Trimingham show Edmund crowned and holding arrows, a proof that the cult of the martyred king lasted into the late Middle Ages. In fact Henry VI (1422-1461), a late comer and saint only by public acclamation, whose piety coupled with the sinister character of his death made him popular, appears on three rood screens in Norfolk at Binham, North Elmham and Barton Turf. The Pope refused to beatify him because Henry VII would not pay the necessary fees.

Choice of Old and New Testament subjects by mediaeval artists appears curiously capricious. Some are widely used, others ignored. Jonah was a favourite subject but never Job; Noah and the Ark but seldom the Crossing of the Red Sea. Parallels between Old and New Testaments seem frequently to be the guiding motive and the moment illustrated is invariably that at which God's intervention was made manifest. On this point the balance of Old Testament types with their Gospel anti-types was carefully planned. Two books summarising these prophetic parallels were among the important sources of mediaeval art. The *Bibliae Pauperum* included only biblical subjects and the slightly later *Speculum Humanae Salvationis* drew on secular history, old Jewish legends and the peculiar lore of bestiary.

To appease men's longing for details of the life of Christ the apocryphal gospels were drawn upon extensively. A boss in the north transept of Norwich Cathedral shows Joseph leading an ox and an ass with the Virgin Mary following. No mention of animals occurs in the New Testament nativity stories. Glass in the east window of St Peter Mancroft, Norwich, depicts Mary giving breast to the Child while the High Priest leans forward to circumcise Him. In the same window we see the Massacre of the Innocents, a child being sliced in two with a scimitar, a mother attempting to strangle a soldier who is murdering her infant, and all taking place in front of Herod enthroned. At East Harling the child Christ is seen seated among the Doctors of the Law who wear caps, gowns and fur lined hoods like Oxford teachers of the period.

The Baptism of Christ, always by affusion, occurs frequently on fourteenth century font panels — at Stalham St Mary for instance where it occupies an opposite panel to the Crucifixion, at Sloley it faces east and it occurs in glass as in St Peter Mancroft. The font, which, after the altar, was focus of the greatest veneration, being of itself the emblem of one of the sacraments, became, towards the end of the fourteenth century a means of stressing their importance. The polygonal character of the bowl lent itself first to a representation of evangelistic emblems (Happisburgh) then to the evangelists themselves or to incidents in Christ's life (Blofield). The glory of the seven sacrament font was finally achieved in the fifteenth century. Of these Norfolk possesses 25 out of the country's total of 40. Most of them received the full force of the reformers' desecration zeal and are sadly mutilated. The best preserved can be seen at Sloley and also at Gresham and Walsoken. All must originally have been coloured and some still retain traces of it. Much of the grace and charm of these fonts is dependent on their aedicular character, miniature vaulting being carried out not only in the panels but in the arched coronas. At Brooke the angels of the corona carry inscribed labels. At Salle the angels hold emblems of the sacraments depicted above them.

East Dereham St Nicholas. Seven Sacrament font, dated 1468. The panels have miniature vaulting and the corners mutilated figures under canopies. Corner shafts die down into seated figures with emblems of the evangelists. The corona is upheld by demi-angels.

Of the miracles only the marriage at Cana appears to have been at all popular. At East Harling the glass shows Mary, crowned as Queen of Heaven, ordering servants to fill pots with water while beside her stands a man with a halo and bearing the palm of martyrdom. The Passion and Resurrection naturally received such emphasis that their representation must have attracted the destructive zeal of the iconoclasts. Despite their efforts much remains. Tormentors press the crown of thorns upon Christ's brow in St Peter Mancroft glass, the Virgin swoons amid a group of women at the Crucifixion on the font at Salle, an angel bears away the soul of the repentant thief in glass at Hingham and the dead Christ lies across the knees of His mourning mother in the window of East Harling.

It should be borne in mind that iconography on screens, benches and bench ends represents a later mediaeval refinement and carries a moral directive beyond the scope of the earlier murals. Secular movements such as chivalry added impetus to the Church's emphasis on gentleness, charity and a more benign attitude towards women that arrived on the heels of the greater veneration of the Virgin. Naturally the iconoclasts fell with fury upon the more obvious examples of this and, other than its representation on inaccessible bosses, little remains than purely domestic scenes, such as the boss in St Helen's Norwich, showing the Virgin about to dry the infant Jesus on a towel while a servant stands by with a basin of gruel.

Apostles, the Four Doctors and the wide Communion of Saints depicted on Norfolk screens have all fared better so long as one can discount the viciousness with which faces on the panels have invariably been mutilated. Norfolk is probably richest of all counties for the beauty of its mediaeval screens. Munro Cautley considers there are no less than 202 churches still possessing screens or remains of them, a statement he follows up with a list emphasising with capitals 100 as being more or less intact to the head. In the fourteenth century screens assumed an elegance seldom attained in earlier work. The fifteenth century saw the culminating perfection of wood, gesso and colour ornament. Not only had figure work become elegant, graceful and free from stylised drapery, but the flower and spray work of the backgrounds and the hollows of the mouldings became delicate and delightful.

Foremost among the saints depicted were those who might be described as the oldest and most popular 'dedication' saints, Andrew, Peter and Paul and John the Baptist. Then follows the "noble army of Martyrs", revered as most potent intercessors before the Throne of God. Both saints and martyrs can be identified by their emblems, St Lawrence with his gridiron, St Andrew with his saltire cross, St Peter's keys, St Paul's sword, St Dorothy with her basket of roses (she is on Walpole St Peter screen) St Barbara with a small tower (at Ranworth), St Catherine with her wheel (North Tuddenham). Local figures go to swell the ever increasing army of saints and martyrs. St Walstan appears on screens at Barnham Broom, Litcham, Ludham, North Burlingham and Sparham and on a chest at Denton. St

William of Norwich is at Litcham and Worstead and his martyrdom is depicted at Loddon.

The Doctors, SS Gregory, Jerome, Ambrose and Augustine of Hippo usually occur only on the doors of screens and only nine screens with doors exist in Norfolk. They appear as well on the panels of fifteenth century pulpits at Burnham Norton and Castle Acre. Whether on screen doors or pulpits the symbolism is clear; their teaching opened men's minds to the meaning of Holy Scripture.

Founders of the monastic orders seemed not so well favoured. St Benedict appears on the screen at Burlingham St Andrew, North Elmham, Great Plumstead and Smallburgh while the stigmatism of St Francis can be seen only on the screen at Hempstead.

Moral teaching, so common a feature of thirteenth century murals, was brought closer to the congregation by the growing popularity of preaching which in turn was probably responsible for bringing seating into the churches. In the late fourteenth century benches and bench ends became common features, and as such, handy vehicles for instruction. In respect of these Norfolk and Suffolk are again richest of counties and the finest examples are scattered widely over both areas. The period was one when men's minds were stretching out beyond the confines of the Middle Ages. The introduction of printing, the widening of the confines of the Old World introduced fresh concepts and broadened the horizons of imagination. Artists gave new dimensions to age-old Nativity scenes and stories culled from the Apocryphal Gospels the corpus of which had been in existence from the third century for, as we have already said, much of the iconography we possess today would have been starved of ideas had it depended solely upon the canon of the New Testament. Travel gave additional impetus to the imagination as the bestiaries of the period show. Tuttington bench ends have among them a dragon attacking a man and an elephant and castle, Upper Sheringham a mermaid with a comb and Nebuchadnezzar eating grass. Great Walsingham possesses a wide range of curious animals. In the chancel at Horning a demon thrusts a man into Hell's mouth and a man struggles with a two-headed serpent. Nonetheless, from a purely iconographical standpoint, the bench ends at Wiggenhall St Germans and St Mary, Forncett St Peter and Bressingham St John the Baptist are probably unequalled among any mediaeval representation of grotesques and peculiar beasts.

Of the veneration of the Rood that rose to prominence in the late fourteenth and fifteenth centuries little evidence remains other than the small turret stairs that ascend on one side or the other of the chancel arch in so many of our churches. A few retain the bressumer or beam that carried the loft as, for example Tunstead St Mary and Sheringham St Mary while at Attleborough St Mary the loft is practically intact. Most remarkably it runs through nave and aisles, its ribbed west coving complete, together with the loft parapet.

Inculcation of the terrors of Hell received enormous emphasis as the iconographer drew upon his rich imagination and carved its horrors upon bench ends, painted them upon Dooms, enlarged upon them in glass and filled the church eaves with frightening gargoyles. It was the contemplation of these frenzied grotesques close at hand, followed by the more detached awareness of the placid beauties of painted saints, martyrs and angels on the screen and then the still more distant view of a richly coloured altar reredos or the translucent loveliness of an east window that gave the church its most telling and powerful moral contrasts.

Abbot Suger of St Denis in France in the twelfth century is reputed to have said, "The dull mind rises to truth through that which is material." It cannot be emphasised more that the church was the sole repository of material beauty that mediaeval man was free to contemplate. All that was precious to him in this life was contained within its walls and it held out promise of everlasting bliss in the next.

Iconography did not disappear with the Reformation. After the Marian effort to restore the Roman Catholic faith iconography changed course and walked in line with the new thinking. The gradual change to the comparative bareness of a meeting house was all part of the conditioning of men's minds cushioning them towards accepting the tempestuous outpourings of the preacher and the singing of "godly hymns" rather than a dependence upon the sweet melodious condolences of the Mass. The rich colour of walls and woodwork, of vestment and stained glass gave place to whitewash, black cassocks and white glass. Even the old fear of Hell had its substitute — an absolute veneration for the majesty of Death. Mural monuments of the late sixteenth century and the early seventeenth century display an inordinate profusion of skulls and crossbones. Not until after the Restoration of the Monarchy in 1661 did chubby little cherubs and fat little weepers begin to supplant the cadavers.

By that time the mediaeval concept of religion was dead. Though sectarian differences were still to remain, the great cleavage was at last obvious. Gone was the priest and his sacraments and only individual man and his conscience remained. What havoc these two created is all too evident.

CHAPTER SEVEN

Furnishing of the Church

IMAGERY and furnishing in the mediaeval church tend to be partners. This is because many of the individual items of furnishing such as fonts, holy water stoups, piscinas and aumbries, even some tombs, possessed iconographic connotations. All became aids to the church's fundamental purpose, the guidance of man's soul to salvation. Unless this is clearly understood we are liable to regard the contents of the mediaeval church as little more than varying degrees of architectural and artistic fashion or just symbolic indications of man's reaching out towards maturity, neither of which is true. After all, what is left for us today has already suffered centuries of scorn and disrespect. It would be the final indignity were it to be treated to the ridicule of ignorance.

We have to accept that many a church had little of interest to commend it at any time and these, together with all the rest, suffered from the hand of the Victorian restorer. Antiquarian and archaeologist combine to deplore the rabid restorations that occurred at the latter end of the nineteenth century. While it must be admitted that the restorers often threw out the baby with the bath water, even so two points have to be considered in mitigation of their efforts. The period was strongly evangelical and a gulf existed between High and Low Church, particularly in Norfolk. Where the Low Church was dominant the restorer was welcomed as one who cleared away "High Church paraphernalia". The other point was the awful heritage of decay and deterioration of fabric due to a hundred or more years of neglect.

Then too fashion ran strong for pitch pine, cast iron, varnished wood and distemper. Ancient oak was eyed with disfavour and the ear of the restorer listened tingling with anticipation for the love call of the death watch beetle as an excuse for the destruction of many a hammer beam roof.

Happily the present mood is for preservation. Today we realise that the church is not only hallowed by the worship of centuries but it has become the silent depository of local history. Beneath its paving sleep generations of squires, their bones occasionally shaken up to make room for their descendents. Outside lie uncoffined and unmarked by epitaph or inscription successive generations of fathers of the hamlet.

In city churches tomb chests, slabs and brasses record our mediaeval merchants. In Norwich we have the Jannys tomb of terracotta in St George

Colegate, the Pettus mural monument in SS Simon and Jude and the Suckling, Rugg and Garsętt tombs in St Andrew, to say nothing of the collection of excellent merchant brasses in St John Maddermarket, St Giles and St Andrew.

About the county occur Gothic tomb chests with or without effigies. To mention but a few here, we have the thirteenth century Purbeck marble effigy of a priest at West Walton, the Kerdiston tomb at Reedham, a late thirteenth century knight at East Tuddenham, the Gerbrigge tombs at Wickhampton and the glorious terracotta Bedingfield tombs at Oxborough. Nor should one leave out the Southwell memorials at Wood Rising and the Morley monument at Hingham (1453) described by Niclaus Pevsner as one of the most ambitious funeral compositions in England. These monuments indicate how the powerful, the wealthy, the ambitious tried to ensure their soul's welfare and the perpetuation of their names. The custom continued after the Reformation and the mural monuments of later centuries will be described in due course.

General mention of these has been made here because in so many churches they are the most prominent of furnishings. Churches tended to become mausoleums. Sometimes the very structure was altered to contain their magnificence. Such an effect can be seen in Felbrigg where a lovely thirteenth century sedilia has been masked by one of the Windham memorials. Memorials of the Coke family completely dominate Tittleshall chancel. They are all extraneous. The true mediaeval furnishings of a church are those that were visible incitements to mediaeval man's worship, and the presence of which was essential to the liturgy of the pre-Reformation church.

What follows is a sketch of these furnishings, grouped as far as possible around the specific purpose for which each was evolved.

The Porch

Though the porch — or narthex — had been a common feature of Saxon churches it was not until the late thirteenth century that porches came once more to be built. Whether the porch represented an advance in comfort is hard to prove. More than likely it was an addition made at the same time as considerable rebuilding was undertaken. It was a period when sacramentally the church became as important as the sacraments performed therein. The old secular uses of the nave as a meeting place, market place, law court were now frowned upon so a porch provided cover outside the hallowed place. Moreover the porch served certain liturgical purposes. Much of the sacrament of baptism and a part of the marriage service were carried out in the porch; the churching of women began there and the penitent received partial absolution at the church door after standing there three consecutive Sundays in a white sheet. Legal activities moved there from the nave and pronouncements of outlawry were made there. It still remains

East Dereham St Nicholas. Perpendicular porch entrance. Note the holy water stoups the flanking canopied and stooled niches and spandrels displaying the Annunciation.

the legal place for displaying public notices which, if the parish prove too par-simonious to put up a notice board, are pinned onto the priceless oak of a lovely pre-Reformation door.

Before long the porch was given more monumental dimensions, being raised to two and sometimes three storeys, the upper serving traditionally as a depository for important records. Finally the church entrance developed into a handsome frontispiece having an ornamental outer arch with a good traceried window above as at Loddon All Saints and Worstead St Mary. The latter porch has three canopied and crocketed mouldings at the entrance and is flush panelled. Inside it is vaulted, the central boss depicting the Trinity. Of note is the late thirteenth century porch at Great Massingham, most impressive with its open arcades and deep mouldings. Equally lovely is the south porch of West Walton St Mary with arcaded, octagonal and pinnacled buttresses and a fine arch on three attached columns, with two rows of dog tooth ornament. Other splendid porches can be seen at Walpole St Peter, Brisley, Cawston, Cley, Colby, East Dereham, North Elmham (an interesting west porch) Fersfield, Gissing, Hellington (thirteenth century with a fine moulded arch with caps and moulded buttresses, each with a canopied niche), Walsoken and Wymondham.

Mass Dials

On many a south porch can still be seen a scratched circle, usually about four inches in diameter with a hole in the centre and a number of radii depending from it. Generally it is on the eastern jamb of the arch, only occasionally on the west and sometimes it occurs on the set-off of a south facing buttress. This circle was a mass dial, the mediaeval priests' only means of dividing the daylight hours into three parts so that he might time the services and give notice of this by tolling the bell. With the coming of clocks in the late fourteenth century the inaccuracy of these dials was revealed and many are found today with other scratches added in efforts made to get the shadow to agree with clock time. In some cases the dial itself was duplicated as can be seen on the priest's door at Worstead, on the south porch of Sprowston and at Trunch.

Some no longer occupy their original position. Repairs probably dislodged them and later, the odd piece of freestone came in for patching another portion of the stonework. At Gissing a dial is on the north-east quoin of the tower, at Cley on the south-west buttress of the south transept while at Forncett St Mary one is inverted on the south-west quoin of the nave.

The Doorway

In Saxon times the doorway possessed all the iconographic significance of the Portal to Heaven. It was this sanctity that later, when porches came to be built,

Haddiscoe St Mary. South doorway with typical Saxon embellishment of arch and jambs.

led to the upper storey being named the parvise, the View of Paradise. I think colouring was originally lavished on the various orders of mouldings particularly on the rich Saxo-Norman patternings. At Cotton in Suffolk some of the mediaeval colouring is still apparent. Though the door's symbolic influence faded with the building of a porch, considerable reverence remained. Evidence of this is seen in the many magnificent mediaeval doors adorned with fine tracery in wood and with majestic wrought iron enfoliated hinges, door handles and striker rings. Graffiti scratched on the door jambs occasionally tell a story less mischievous than pious. They can be indications of a successful return from pilgrimage as, for example, the double crosses at Swafield St Nicholas. At Aylmerton a minute arrow and embattlement cut on the west cap of the doorway speaks of the original Lord of the Manor, John of Gaunt, Duke of Lancaster.

Apart from the many Saxo-Norman doors of distinction Norfolk has a wealth of mediaeval doors and doorways. Before all else stand West Walton and Cley and following closely is East Tuddenham. For craftsmanship in wood Billingford, Brooke and New Buckenham are outstanding while Tunstead stands supreme for the remarkable ironwork radiating from a central boss, said to be of Flemish origin.

The Font

Second only to the altar, the font is the most venerated of all church furnishing. Its association with the sacrament of baptism and the antiquity of the custom both contribute to its sanctity. Earliest baptisms were adult, conducted by a bishop in a pool or stream. Sites of churches were frequently positioned close to a holy well, a stream or pool as at East Dereham. In fact early baptisteries were detached from the church as was originally the case at Canterbury. Growth of parochial organisation led to the local priest deputising for the bishop. So, a font became a necessary feature of every church. At first its position was in the narthex or porch and throughout the Middle Ages most of the ritual of baptism took place outside the church. This accounts for the font being always at the west end close to whatever entrance came commonly to be used.

The sanctity of the font led to a wonderful diversity in their appearance and a wide development of ornament. The Saxo-Norman tub font, whether rectangular or tub shaped, carries typical Saxon designs. That at Little Snoring has scroll work not quite so perfect as at Deerhurst, Gloucestershire. A definite group of square faced tub fonts in West Norfolk comprises Toftrees, Sculthorpe, Shernborne, Breccles, Burnham Deepdale and Castle Rising. Their ornament makes them some of the most magnificent fonts of the period in England. That at Burnham Deepdale, below a frieze of lions, on three of its faces depicts the monthly occupations throughout the year. Toftrees has intricate scrollwork and at the corners beak-like heads. Sculthorpe, more maturely carved, bears apostle figures beneath

Little Snoring St Andrew. Saxon font with typical scroll ornamentation around the circular bowl.

interlaced arcades while, finest of all, Shernborne, is a mass of rich carving with shafts, spirally cut, and capitals at the corners, interlacing work between the plaited bands at the top and four grotesque faces at the base. Not far off, Fincham has figures under the arches, on the east the three Magi, to the south the Nativity with manger, ox, ass and Joseph, to the north Adam and Eve.

Following this remarkable artistic output, the thirteenth century plainness of Purbeck marble fonts seems retrogressive. These have become hexagonal or octagonal, their faces decorated with blank pointed arch arcading, either two or three to each face. This common ornament leads to the supposition that all were rough-cut at the quarry face and transported in coastal vessels as ballast, borne out by the fact that the forty-one Purbeck marble fonts found in Norfolk are all near the coast or near navigable rivers, estuaries and creeks. At the time they probably represented wealth planted gem-like amid the dim starkness of the small Saxo-Norman church: Beighton, Burnham Thorpe, Easton, Filby, Ingham, Mattishall Burgh, Moulton and Stody are good examples picked from Norfolk's collection.

Thereafter fashion changed, Purbeck marble was no longer wanted and the fourteenth century began to see the familiar shaped, typical East Anglian font, finest of all being that at Yaxham. It has a traceried bowl with coved vaulting under an ogee arch, cinquefoiled with shields beneath. Ovington has angels blossoming from shields, Stalham comes late in the century and is allegorical and more austere. Blofield is unique in that it depicts scenes from the life of Christ.

The crowning glory of the pre-Reformation church was the fifteenth century Seven Sacrament Font of which Norfolk possesses 25, Suffolk 13, Kent and Somerset one each. A few are products of the sixteenth century, for example Walsoken, as late as 1544. So important are these that I include the whole list, italicising those that are the least mutilated. Alderford, Binham, Brooke, Burgh St Mary, Cley, South Creake, East Dereham, Earsham, Gayton Thorpe, Gorleston, *Gresham,* Loddon, West Lynn, Marsham, Martham, Norwich St Peter Mancroft, Norwich Cathedral, *Salle,* Seething, *Sloley,* Walpole St Peter, Little Walsingham, *Walsoken,* Wendling, Great Witchingham.

Most of these, because they emphasised not only baptism but all the sacraments of the Roman Church, were severely mutilated at the Reformation. Many have magnificent traceried and panelled steps (Loddon and Little Walsingham have a third step shaped like a Maltese cross on which stood the god-parents) and all must originally have been coloured for several retain traces of this.

Inscription on fonts is sufficiently common for mention to be made here and particularly as many are difficult to decipher. The most common, a Greek palindrome — a phrase which reads the same from either end — is, in translation: "Wash my sins and not my face only" and can be seen on Knapton font. Round the base of Acle St Edmund font are the words: "Orate pro animabus qui istum fontem in honore dei fiere fecerunt, Anno Dmi. Millimo cccc decimo." Similar inscriptions occur at Saham Toney, Salle, South Acre, Tilney All Saints and Walsoken.

There was a marked deterioration in post-Reformation veneration for the church seen not only in general mutilation of fonts. It was indeed a period of disorder and indecency, its ultimate limits held in check only by occasional episcopal efforts, not always successful. For example Bishop Wren of Norwich in 1631 had to make the order that " . . . the font be filled with clean water and no dishes, pails or basons be used in it or instead of it."

In the fifteenth century the font cover had become an elaborate feature of many a church. Fonts had always been kept locked for the double purpose of cleanliness and for checking the use of the water for superstitious purposes. On many, evidence of this is clear by the presence of a metal hasp — or a broken part of the rim where it once existed. But now were erected lofty tabernacled covers, masterpieces of the joiners' and painters' crafts. At Castle Acre, North Walsham,

Fifteenth Century font.

Worstead, Brancaster and Salle they rise like miniature painted spires, rich with canopy work and with buttresses pinnacled and crocketed. The cover at Terrington St Clement is fitted with doors which on being opened reveal paintings depicting the Baptism of Christ, two scenes from the Temptation and many Latin and English inscriptions.

There are few post-Reformation fonts in the country and it seems that enthusiasm for Classical art and the influence of Inigo Jones and Sir Christopher Wren crept in both slowly and sparsely. At Gaywood is an octagonal Perpendicular font with seventeenth century inscriptions, a seventeenth century bowl at Tilney All Saints and eighteenth century baluster fonts at Anmer, Croxton, Northwold, Warham All Saints and North Runcton.

I have the feeling that many a fine mediaeval font cover disappeared during the sixteenth century, probably at the time the fonts themselves were mutilated. In their place abound many a seventeenth century cover, at least seven in Norwich alone. Of the large number in the county the best are at Knapton (1704), Wiggenhall St Mary the Virgin (1625) and Watlington (c. 1620).

The Altar

From earliest days the altar was the chief object of adoration, essential to the perfection of the liturgy. In Anglo Saxon terms it was God's Board and its man-ifestation in wood continued on till the end of the eleventh century. Later pre-Reformation mensas were commonly of stone incised with the five consecration crosses. Norfolk possesses a few of these, at Hanworth, Larling and Weston Longville. At Eccles is a mensa 9′ 8″ by 3′ 6″, an unusual size. In the Jesus Chapel of Norwich Cathedral the mensa has its "seal of the altar", a square of Purbeck marble let in to cover a space originally containing relics. In Terrington St Clement are three mensas and at Forncett St Peter, one, now acting as paving stones. It is usually thought that Elizabeth I ordered their destruction; her injunction permitted their abolition but did not command it and she required that a "decent table" be substituted. In consequence there can be seen fine Tudor and Stuart tables serving as altars in many churches, in all nearly two hundred. Best Elizabethan tables are at Beeston Regis, Clenchwarton, South Acre and West Winch. Elizabethan tables had enormous, bulbous, highly carved legs and generally both top and bottom rails carried carving. In James I's reign legs were still bulbous but less elaborate and with the years they became steadily lighter in construction and less ornate.

Altar rails may fairly be said to be Laudian, dating from the latter part of Charles I's reign. In 1623 Bishop Wren of Norwich ordered that "The Rayle be . . . near one yard in height, so thick with pillars that doggs may not get in." Many were destroyed during the Commonwealth but following the Restoration of the Monarchy and the Episcopate in 1660 they were put back and thereafter became a common feature of church furniture. Some Laudian rails still exist at South Burlingham and Lingwood while at Potter Heigham they have been cut in two and placed in front of the choir seats. At St. Gregory Norwich "VI great posts and forty two pillars were provided".

The wall behind the altar was in some cases treated architecturally to form a reredos. Little remains of these in the county. Two High Gothic niches mark the north and south extremes of what could have been one at Tunstead behind a mysterious and singular raised platform. Two small aedicular pieces in the wall of this could be part of a once handsome piece of work. Three sculptured alabaster panels still exist in Norwich, at St Peter Mancroft, St Stephens and in the Cathedral Chapter House. These are thought to be part of a reredos in the Chapel of St Mary's College, totally destroyed at the Reformation.

The Retable in St Luke's Chapel in the Cathedral is an excellent example of what was probably a common practice in England. It is the work of artists of the Norwich School at the latter end of the fourteenth century. It consists of five boards fastened together with a moulded frame pinned in front. Its subjects are the Passion and include the Flagellation, the Way of the Cross, the Crucifixion, the Resurrection and the Ascension. To commemorate the local defeat of the Peasants' Revolt, Bishop Henry Le Despenser, Stephen Hales and Sir Thomas Morieux ordered it as a gift to the Cathedral.

Eccles St Mary. Large stone mensa on modern supports.

Ludham: richly cusped, crocketed, and pinnacled piscina and graduated sedilia separated by attached shafts.

Piscina and Sedilia

Piscina is the name given to a particular water drain sited near the altar. It is commonly to be found at a convenient height in the south east corner of the chancel and where there were side chapels in similar arrangement with the side altar. The piscina is built into the wall beneath a niche, moulded and vaulted according to the period of erection.

In A.D. 850 Pope Leo directed that a place be provided for disposal of water used in the cleansing of the sacred vessels and the priest's hands. In the thirteenth century the washing of hands before the Canon of the Mass was enjoined, so there came about two drains and basins side by side. A century later the celebrant was expected to drink the ablutions — a highly improbable idea — but it is the only theory advanced for a return to the single drain.

Fine examples of double piscina can be seen at Carlton Rode, Baconsthorpe, Besthorpe and Pulham St Mary. At Trunch and at Hempstead are small enclosed lockers on the west side of the piscina which were used for the cruets.

Sedilia, more often than not an extension to the west of the piscina, were the three stone seats, or recesses and canopied stalls intended for the priest, the deacon and the sub-deacon officiating at High Mass. The more ornate examples are graduated in height, the priest using the highest and nearest the east. In many Norfolk churches the sill of the window in the south wall of the chancel is lowered to form an inexpensive kind of sedilia bench.

Fine canopied and vaulted sedilia are at Tunstead, Ludham and Felbrigg. The aedicular work at Tunstead is particularly charming. Felbrigg has unfortunately been masked by memorials. At Besthorpe the fourteenth century sedilia has pedimented and crocketed heads with cusped ogee tracery below.

Easter Sepulchres

In mediaeval days the Easter Sepulchre held the same interest as does the Christmas Crib today, and infinitely more veneration. It was a movable chest or receptacle fitting a niche usually on the north side of the chancel. On Maundry Thursday the pyx containing a consecrated wafer, a cross from the altar and probably a figure of Christ were reverently placed in the sepulchre and all put into the niche. Watch was kept night and day until Easter Sunday when the contents were replaced on the altar. So was enacted the Death and Resurrection of Christ before the people.

This was not all. The sepulchre was hung with costly hangings and adorned with flowers and gifts and these together with the empty tomb remained in position for another week. As far as is known none of the original wooden structures has survived. The importance for us lies in the vestiges of evidence remaining, the few niches and, more important still, the tombs that can often be found on the north side of the chancel which clearly provided a resting place for the sepulchre.

The finest Easter Sepulchre in Norfolk is at Northwold, a lavish fifteenth century composition that has suffered badly from mutilation and neglect. Against the base, in attitudes of fear, sit soldiers, separated from each other by little trees. To left and right are buttresses. Above is a top cresting and the recess has vaulting in two tiers.

Numerous recesses still exist, notably that at Ranworth. A tomb on the south side of Tasburgh chancel has all the characteristics of one. Undoubtedly the great Morley tomb at Hingham served originally as a resting place for an Easter Sepulchre. Other obvious recesses can be seen at Baconsthorpe, Blakeney, North Creake, Kelling and Raveningham.

Church Plate

As has been said in an earlier chapter, the Reformation made a clean sweep of the sacred vessels used in the liturgy of the Mass. By the accession of Elizabeth I churches had been left with only one chalice and one paten each. Pre-Reformation chalices were expropriated wholesale because, when all the laity partook of Communion a much larger cup was called for than when only the celebrant priest took the Sacrament. In consequence, in all Norfolk, while there are 34 pre-Reformation patens in existence, only St Peter Mancroft, Norwich owns a chalice. When Archbishop Parker made his visitation in 1569 he asked, *inter alia,* "Whether they do minister in any prophane cuppes, bowles, dishes, or chalices heretofore used at Masse; or els in a decent Communion cuppe provided and kept for that purpose." The Elizabethan cup at Thornage bears the inscription, "This is ye gyfte of John Bates and Margaret hys wyfe, 1456, whych died 1477." On the paten cover of this cup appears "The fashon altred by I. Stalom, d. a 1563."

A great number of Elizabethan chalices exists and it is a wonder how the silversmiths of the period managed to cope with the sudden demand put upon them. Perhaps the situation was eased by gifts. Norwich St Andrews owns two fine seventeenth century standing cups which are clearly secular in character.

At an early post-Reformation date flagons became important. Invariably they were in pairs. It is noticeable that these, whether in silver or pewter, increased in number and popularity after the Restoration of the Monarchy in 1660. In the course of years they were to become an accepted part of Nonconformist chapel plate. The Octagon Chapel, Norwich, for example possesses six patens and four chalices dated 1713.

Stalls and Misericords

The Saxo-Norman custom that raised the Bishop's Throne — the Cathedra — in the centre apse behind the altar at Norwich was never to become common to England, probably because the cruciform church was not generally adopted and elongated chancels became the rule. As a result the clergy was early transferred from stalls around the apse to the western portion of the choir extending — in monastic foundations — one or more bays into the nave. Clergy stalls were grouped on each side the choir in one or two rows with return stalls at the west. The two nearest the entrance under the pulpitum were always reserved for the Abbot and Prior. This arrangement was copied by the great collegiate foundations and later by parish churches wealthy enough to support both priest and deacons as, for example, Tilney All Saints, Walpole St Peter and Walsoken.

Misericords, the "Mercy Seats" so designed as to give some slight rest for those suffering from the long hours of the monastic offices, varied in number according to the size and importance of the foundation. Norwich had sixty-two. At first they were reserved solely for monastic and collegiate foundations but by the late fourteenth century had become a feature of the larger parish churches. Because East Anglia had by then become the industrial centre of the country Norfolk shares with her sister counties the distinction of being wealthy enough to have more than any other part of the country. A feature of the carving on misericords is the strong sense of realistic humour particularly associated with retributive justice. In Norwich Cathedral Greed slips drunk from a sow's back spilling his ale; a lion mauls a man; a woman chases a fox that has stolen her goose. In the early ones the emphasis is on the conquest of evil; the later ones tend to be more comic and worldly.

Norwich Cathedral misericord: man spearing griffin.

Norwich Cathedral misericord: owl, which preferred to remain in the darkness of its misbelief, mobbed by small birds.

Norwich cathedral misericord. Christ wins back sinners to grace by showing His wounds as a hawk is lured back by the falconer with raw meat, the falcon here is the symbol of Christ wounded.

Other than the Cathedral some of the best can be seen at Aylsham (1507), Binham, Blakeney, Castle Acre, Cawston (c. 1460), Cley, East Harling, King's Lynn St Margaret (c. 1420), Norwich, SS Andrew, Michael Coslany, Gregory, Peter Mancroft, North Walsham, Salle, Trunch, Thompson, Tilney All Saints. At Walpole St Peter five misericords are under stone canopies and rest upon stone supports.

Screens and Rood Lofts

Mediaeval England was pre-eminently the land where the rood screen most predominated. Many and lovely are the surviving examples, particularly in East Anglia and the West Country. The screen was a practical means whereby the mystery of the chancel or sacrarium was maintained. In Saxon times the narrow chancel opening beneath the central tower of the tripartite or cruciform church was undoubtedly screened with a veil. As the more open view of the chancel according to the later Western church gained ground in England there came first the triple arched stone chancel screens of the thirteenth century, survivals of which are in Norwich Cathedral, Wymondham and Ingham.

The stone screen disappeared in favour of wood in the late fourteenth century. From then onwards beautiful timber screenwork coved at the top and with beams to support a wide rood loft became the fashion.

It is hard to decide just when veneration of the Rood became an important part of worship. Probably monastic in origin the fashion caught on throughout the following half century. In a number of cases it was the reason for blocking up an earlier east window above the chancel arch. Where the original screen was low, or the chancel arch tall, the beam carrying the Rood was placed above the summit of the screen as at Tunstead. Instances of corbels formerly carrying the rood beam are very numerous.

Destruction of Roods at the Reformation was demanded throughout the country but the screen was invariably left undisturbed. Consequently the county remains the proud possessor of 202 churches having screens or the remains of screens. They occur chiefly as screens before the chancel with, in a lesser number of cases parclose screens as well which probably, in pre-Reformation days, enclosed chantry chapels.

Though differing considerably in final design, the basic arrangement is similar, namely, a solid base, divided into panels by uprights or buttresses supporting a stage of openwork. This is divided into compartments by shafts or mullions with tracery in the heads of the divisions and completed by an enriched beam, cornice or coving. The centre division formed the entrance to the chancel. Of all Norfolk's screens only nine are fitted with doors. However doors could have been fitted against the mouldings so that the only evidence would be the hinge fittings which could easily have been re-tooled away as at Lessingham and St Peter Hungate, Norwich.

In the later fourteenth century screens began to assume elegance. Examples of this period can be found at Thompson, Watlington, Edingthorpe, and slightly later ones at Holme Hale and Merton. Onwards from then until the Reformation screens progressed in colour decoration, skill in construction and in ingenuity of design. At Gooderstone are lofty buttresses with muntins and image brackets. Ludham has remarkable detached pinnacles to the buttresses, rising from fine bases and cleverly linked to give strength.

Though many are now bare oak, in their day most were coloured. However, there are still some eighty Norfolk churches possessing painted panels. Of these twenty-two depict saints. At Barton Turf the south aisle screen carries pictures of kingly saints. Most panels have series of saints ordained by and in an order demanded by the iconography of the day.

It would be impossible at this point to mention all the notable screens in the county. But, for beauty of workmanship and artistry, those of Ranworth, Tunstead, Ludham, Cawston and Worstead call for special attention.

Lecterns

It was the mediaeval custom to have reading desks in the chancel from which to read the Gospels. At first they were of wood, later of metal and were movable. Very occasionally a fixed one of stone was used. The Reformed Church brought the lectern out into the body of the nave for the general reading of the Lessons.

The simple wooden desk is the earlier form, either single, twofold or fourfold. That at Ranworth has a slender stem supporting two desks, one above the other, one painted with a plainsong setting of the Gloria, the other with the eagle of St John. A simple fourfold desk on four legs is at Tibenham but this looks suspiciously Jacobean. The finest wooden lectern in the county is at Shipdham, a richly carved oaken double desk resting on a shaft of three buttresses with columns of little quatrefoils in the angles between and three lions at the base. Not quite so ornate is the one at Shelton.

Of metal lecterns Niclaus Pevsner considers East Anglia to have been a centre of export. Examples occur as far away as St Marks, Venice, at Urbino Cathedral and in England at Exeter and Newcastle. Norfolk has eleven, the most notable being Oxborough (1489), Norwich St Gregory (1496) and Wiggenhall St Mary (1518). Norwich Cathedral lectern is a pelican in its piety.

The coved stone bracket once supporting a wooden pulpit in Walpole St Andrew is the only example of its kind in the county. On the south side of the chancel arch, it is approached from the rood stairs. Another stone lectern is against the east wall of the south chapel in Walsoken All Saints.

Shipdham: fifteenth century oak lectern.

Norwich St Gregory. Brass lectern, East Anglian, 1496.

Pulpits and Hour Glasses

Sermons had been the one form of public speech for which English was used by educated men during the years when Latin and French were the dominant languages. The coming of the Friars in the thirteenth century changed the character of sermons and a great increase in their popularity was the result. There followed the introduction of seating in the naves in the latter part of the fourteenth century and the erection of pulpits.

Nearly all pre-Reformation pulpits are similar in appearance, chalice shaped, consisting of an octagonal or hexagonal box with panelled sides set upon a slender stem with miniature buttresses. In Norfolk they are frequently coloured and gilded, and the panels have painted figures of Evangelists or the Doctors of the Church.

The finest among the many pre-Reformation pulpits in the county is in South Burlingham St Edmund. It is fifteenth century with painted panels, traceried and crocketed and its top and bottom rails are each cut from one piece of wood, not jointed as would be customary today. Other notable examples are at Bressingham, Burnham Norton, Castle Acre, South Creake and North Walsham. At Salle the pulpit has been incorporated in a seventeenth century three decker.

The county is again rich in seventeenth century pulpits, among the earliest of which is that of Cley (1611), Necton (a sumptuous piece of 1636 with back panel and tester) and North Elmham (1626 inscribed "Verbum Dei manet in aeternum".)

An important feature of the seventeenth century pulpit was the tester or soundboard, set up by intricate joinery like a great table top above the preacher's head. There are worthwhile specimens of these in Scoulton and Tibenham. In Fincham and St Peter Mancroft, Norwich the old tester is now a vestry table.

The hour glass could have been introduced into some churches before the Reformation. They became an essential when later it was customary for sermons to last an hour and over. There are at least eight hour glass brackets surviving in the county but I know of none still retaining the hour glass in its wooden stand.

Seats and Benches

In early times worshippers stood or knelt for general seating in churches was unknown. Stone benches along the walls in the form of dropped sills or around the base of piers and pillars were an occasional luxury for the old and infirm, probably giving rise to the expression, "The weakest go to the wall." These low sill seats can still be seen at Tunstead, Snettisham and Wiveton. Not until the sermon became an important part of worship towards the end of the fourteenth century did benches become a common feature of church interiors. At first a clear space was left in front of the screen for nave altars, and the acting of morality and nativity plays and there was a clear space left at the west end around the font.

Cawston St Agnes: fifteenth century backless benches in the south aisle.

Benches and bench ends were fitted into a heavy curb. It is thought that the space between these curbs was filled with rushes, a small comfort, for backs were low, formed of a pierced and traceried plank let into a moulded rail. Seats in the aisles often had no backs.

Wonderful craftsmanship was lavished on bench ends, particularly in East Anglia, the finest of all being the shouldered type. Hardly any two are alike. Many have an eastern projection, beginning as an arm rest but eventually becoming the medium for further iconographic treatment. The poppy head of the fleur de lys pattern is the commonest form of head and in some of these is seen a means of making them symbolic. Many bear heads enfoliated with the leaf work or the fundamental triangular shape allowed for variety as in Norwich St Helens where

St Margaret of Antioch tramples upon a dragon wreathed around her feet. Often the bench end below the poppy head came to be enriched not only with chamfering but with figures in niches as at Wiggenhall St Mary the Virgin.

The little church of Irstead St Michael is seated throughout with fifteenth century benches and South Walsham St Mary is practically complete. In Sea Palling St Margaret are fourteen old benches with good poppy heads. At Wimbotsham is an array of ends and arm rests with figures from a bestiary, a chained antelope, a basilisk, a griffon and on the front bench a friar telling his beads. Possibly the most complete set are the sixteenth century benches at Bressingham which retain their curb and are finely carved. There are some interesting ones at Forncett St Peter but the most satisfying of all can be seen at Great Walsingham where they fill the church. Though plainer than some they have delightful traceried and pierced backs, high curbs and in a few cases, interesting arm rests. Others worthy of interest can be seen at Gooderstone, Wilton, Upper Sheringham, Thurgarton and South Burlingham.

Norwich St Helen. Ornamented poppy heads. Fifteenth century. The first depicts St Margaret of Antioch.

Pew and Galleries

After the Reformation the custom of reserving pews became fashionable although condemned by many churchmen. Bishop Corbett of Norwich in 1623 said in a sermon, "Stately pews have now become tabernacles with rings and curtains to them. They want nothing but beds to hear the Word of God in; we have casements, locks and keys and cushions." And Pepys in his Diary records that one day he was fain to stay at his pew door because the sexton had not opened it.

Squires' pews in the county became ostentatious. They were the successors of the old chantry parcloses within which had stood an altar with room for the celebrant and one or two *prie dieus* for the founder and his dame and later their descendants. When chantries were abolished the Lord of the Manor retained the space for his own dignified worshipping. During the following century many fifteenth century benches disappeared in favour of box pews. Worstead possesses a complete set with high back walls as protection from draughts. This form of pew remained a fashionable feature of churches until well into the nineteenth century. Bylaugh is a delightful example of a small church entirely seated with box pews in oak, each lighted with a brass candle holder of the same period.

In Saxon times galleries were a common feature approached by stairs outside the walls. Very occasionally a Saxon wall can reveal a blocked up, unsplayed aperture that could have been the outside entrance to a once existent gallery. I think this could be the case in the north wall of Beeston St Lawrence.

Galleries were forgotten until the late fifteenth century. Of this period we have some for bell ringing, for example St Peter Mancroft, St Gregory and St Michael Coslany, Norwich and a small, restored watching gallery approached from the parvise at Acle. Then there are the two wooden galleries in Worstead and Aylsham. Galleries came strongly into fashion with the Puritan preaching influence. Bishop Montague, in his Articles of Enquiry for the Norwich Diocese, dated 1638 asks, "Is your church scaffolded everywhere or in part? Do those scaffolds so annoy any man's seat or hinder the lights of any window in the church?"

In the eighteenth century western galleries were frequently used for choirs and instrumental accompaniment. (See Thomas Hardy's description of the Mellstock band in his novel *Under the Greenwood Tree*.) Eventually galleries extended themselves above the aisles of the nave often damaging the fabric and certainly obscuring the light. Only one Norwich church, St Saviour, still maintains its western gallery.

Until 1881 the Octagon Chapel had box pews throughout but these were cut down to their present level using the old oak. The little Presbyterian chapel at Hapton has retained the box pews beneath the galleries as they were built in 1750.

Stained Glass

Stained glass early took its place in the iconographical pattern of the mediaeval church. It lent itself favourably to the great schemes of pictorial teaching that had already begun to emblazon walls and screens from the early fourteenth century. Its translucent vividness of colour and detail was something never before achieved in any other medium.

It is impossible to say whether any use was made of glass in Saxon times. Certainly none earlier than the thirteenth century remains and of this most is in the form of scattered fragments. Christopher Woodforde admits that the Norfolk glass of this period is similar in quality and design to contemporary glass in other parts of the country.

This apart, Norfolk is outstanding for the beauty of its glass. Three important types are to be found; first and by far the most important group is the mediaeval glass of the thirteenth to the sixteenth century. Then comes foreign glass of the fifteenth and sixteenth centuries imported into the county in the nineteenth century, some of which, as at Hingham St Andrew, Erpingham St Mary and Warham St Mary comes from the cloister glazing of the German monastery of Steinfeld. The third group includes the numerous fine modern windows to be found in the country.

Thirteenth century roundels in Oxborough R.C. church, four roundels at Saxlingham Nethergate St Mary and a small trefoil in Carlton Rode All Saints reveal Norfolk's early links with the continent. Disorganisation created by the Black Death broke up the old intercommunity of Western Europe and encouraged the establishing of local schools of production. Greys and browns of earlier grisaille gave place to a growing desire for line and detail. Use of a yellow stain was developed, tints became softer, borders more formal and draughtsmanship was improved. A great improvement in canopy work accompanied this and by the fifteenth century came an elaborate use of perspective. In some cases we can see the influence of other forms of art providing a link between glass design and the illumination of manuscripts. For example a figure of St Barnabus in Downham Market St Edmund is similar to one depicted in a psalter of c.1300 made in Ramsey Abbey in whose patronage was the church at that time.

In Mileham St John the Baptist the fourteenth century glass in the west window is almost complete. That formerly in the east window of Elsing St Mary, and spoken of by Blomefield, commemorated Sir Hugh Hastings and its glass illustrated the Annunciation, Nativity, Crucifixion and the Assumption. Other noteworthy examples of fourteenth century glass can be seen at Bale All Saints, Gooderstone St George, Mautby SS Peter and Paul, Gt Walsingham St Peter, Ketteringham St Peter, Shimpling St George and North Elmham St Mary the Virgin.

No complete picture of fifteenth century glass in Norfolk exists owing to the difficulty of putting the surviving remains into any sort of chronological order. Some of the Saxlingham Nethergate glass is datable to c.1400 and fragments at Salle S.S. Peter and Paul and Litcham All Saints are c.1410-1420. Style of the large panels at North Tuddenham St Mary and some pieces at Cawston St Agnes suggest a date between 1420-1430 and that at W. Rudham St Peter, Narborough All Saints and Ketteringham St Peter belong probably to the next decade. Glazing at Salle and Norwich St Peter Mancroft, established a distinctive Norwich style which happily continued and developed to the end of the century.

Development of this Norwich style is carried forward and the Mancroft idiom appears at East Harling SS Peter and Paul and later still at Pulham St Mary the Virgin, Martham St Mary and Mulbarton St Mary Magdalene.

Of sixteenth century glass some of the best and most distinctive can be seen at Shelton St Mary, Outwell St Clement, and Norwich St Stephen and St Andrew. The glass of St Peter Mancroft and of Harling SS Peter and Paul demand especial mention. In the former are 42 panels (only 7 of which are modern), in the latter the window is complete. In both cases the glass must have been cherished and preserved in troublous times. Both great windows are the work of unknown artists and glass painters of a Norwich School previously referred to which rose to fame in the fifteenth century. Their work shows a humanitarian approach, the use of contemporary dress and settings and the vivid use of canopy work and colour. Moreover evidence points to an influence emanating from the guild plays of the period for many scenes seem remarkably like stage settings.

That there existed a close link between all forms of imagery within the church is abundantly clear. Where reasonably complete windows remain they point to the possibility of the whole church conforming to an overall iconographic programme. This is what Elsing St Mary must have been in the mid fourteenth century, Salle SS Peter and Paul and Wiggenhall St Mary Magdalene in the fifteenth century and Shelton St Mary in the sixteenth century.

It is during the last mentioned century that much heraldic treatment was developed. Aylsham St Michael south chancel and the east windows of Shelton St Mary are examples of this. Donors had their portraits incorporated within the general heraldic design.

Gothic revival of the nineteenth century gave a new impetus to design and workmanship of stained glass. William Morris and the Pre-Raphaelite movement influenced the work filling it with a feeling for purer design. The complete range of windows in Booton St Michael is typical of the best of that century. Unfortunately a great amount of glass of the period fails dismally to reach anything near the high standards attained earlier.

Parish Chests

Chests, coffers and hutches were the most common, movable pieces of mediaeval domestic furniture. Naturally they, or their counterpart found their way into churches for the safe keeping of valuables and vestments. The oldest form was the dug-out, made by gouging out a solid block of wood. Some of this type remaining today could easily be of Saxon origin. Two examples of them can be seen at Horning and Shipdham.

Variety creeps in once the primitive form was passed over. Then the commonest form consisted of heavy slabs of oak bound with iron. Sometimes the ironwork assumed lively foliation of design as at Hoveton St John or could completely cover the chest as in Blickling, Gimingham, Salle and Wickmere. Midway between the two types quoted occurs the Hindringham chest, most certainly Norman in origin. The front consists of two broad upright boards with rosettes and three horizontal boards framed in, with one row of tall intersected arches.

Hindringham St Martin. The chest is reputed to be of Norman origin.

The third type, dating from the fourteenth century, is panelled and carved without any particular ironwork. No finer example in the county could be found than that at Wilton. In Dersingham is a chest carved in front with the names of the Evangelists. The lid when complete bore an inscription around its border in Lombardic capitals, part written backwards.

The sixteenth century introduced variety in chest decoration. Some are adorned with scenes in poker work — Ashwellthorpe and Great Witchingham. At Fersfield is a yew chest with incised patterning and at Redenhall is one richly carved with inlaid panels, probably from Gawdy Hall.

From then onwards, later chests conform to the usual panelled Jacobean and Carolean pattern.

Poor Man's Boxes and Offertory Boxes

The county possesses a number of Poor Man's Boxes, a few of which can be dated as pre-Reformation. Whatever their age they are more often than not rough hewn and many-banded in iron and could easily be the work of the village carpenter and blacksmith. Their mediaeval use is somewhat cloudy and was certainly not associated with relief of the poor. It is more than probable that they were used for such projects as the Crusades or for the collection of Peter's Pence, the annual tribute of a silver penny per household for the support of the Papacy.

Their use as a direct means of collecting money for the poor dates from the second half of the sixteenth century. Many were dated then and in the following century. Both Edward VI and Elizabeth I enjoined parishioners to help the poor as generously as possible.

At Loddon we have what is reputed to be a Saxon poor man's box. The carved figure of a beggar serves as one at Watton (1639) and at Ludham is the cut-out trunk of a tree heavily banded with iron and carrying four padlocks (1450?).

It is doubtful whether offertory boxes were in use in the Middle Ages. The Tithes as well as other gifts were more likely to be in kind rather than in coin. The First Reformed Prayer Book of the Church of England (1549) provided for certain sentences to be sung "whiles the people doo offer". A later rubric ordered that alms be collected "in a decent bason to be provided by the parish" and wardens were to "reverently bring it up to the priest." (1662).

Royal Arms

The exhibiting of Royal Arms in churches originated by government order in the reign of Henry VIII to mark the cleavage from Rome. Many examples remain from the seventeenth and eighteenth centuries but of the few existing Tudor emblems Norfolk has three of Elizabeth I, at Kenninghall St Mary, Ludham St

Catherine and Tivetshall St Mary. That at Ludham is inscribed "Non me pudit Evangelium Christi" (I am not ashamed of Christ's Gospel) and "Vivat Regina Elizabethi". Tivetshall's Royal Arms is undoubtedly the finest in the country and fills the whole tympanum above the screen but alas, it is so dirty as to be almost impossible to decipher.

It is clear that the Commonwealth dealt harshly with these emblems of the Monarchy but a few others remain from that period. At Tacolneston All Saints the Arms of James I have been re-inscribed for Charles I and dated 1610. In North Walsham is a set of Arms of Charles II on one side and on the other a Commonwealth device, (the cross of St George and the harp of Ireland enwreathed on the dexter side with a palm leaf, on the sinister side with an olive branch). Many specimens of subsequent reigns exist, ranging from elaborately carved sets like those of William III above the tower arch in Shelton St Mary to almost indecipherable devices crudely stained on boards at Toft Monks. The Arms of Anne are numerous, probably installed as a mark of esteem by the clergy for her restitution under the name of Queen Anne's Bounty of endowments filched from them in 1534.

Tivetshall St Margaret. The finest Royal Arms of Elizabeth I in existence.

By courtesy of Eastern Counties Newspapers.

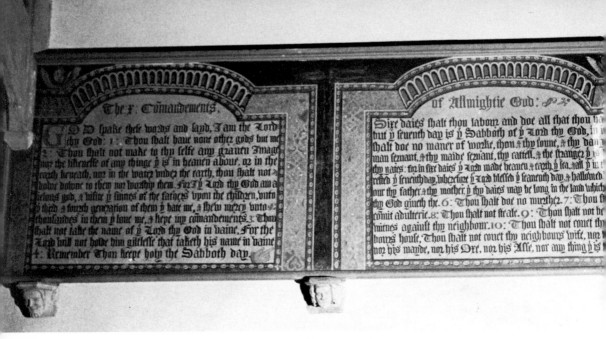

Shipdham All Saints. Elizabethan Commandment Boards.

Commandment and Creed Boards

In 1560 Elizabeth I wrote to the Ecclesiastical Commissioners of the day complaining of the desolate and unclean condition of many churches. They were ordered to set up Tables of the Commandments, not only to be read but "to give some comely ornament and demonstrate that the same was a place of religion and prayer".

Shipdham still has its Elizabethan Boards of the Creed and Commandments. Many in the course of years have come to be relettered. Two fine examples of eighteenth century work are at Wood Rising (flanked by large paintings of Moses and Aaron) and at Norwich St Helen. The latter also possesses two Georgian hymn boards, probably the only ones in the county.

Chandeliers and Candelabra

While it is accepted that at least the chancels came to be lighted with candles and candelabra in pre-Reformation days, there was always the Rowell or corona of lights before the Rood. Altar candles had come into general use at the beginning of the thirteenth century. The usual number was two and those candlesticks that remain are in all instances in pairs.

After the introduction of benches and bench ends with the growth of importance of the sermon it is possible that naves were occasionally candle lit.

Most fifteenth and sixteenth poppyheads have holes in the top into which could have been fitted prickets for candles.

In the eighteenth century the fashion set in for lighting the church with brass chandeliers bearing two tiers of branched candlesticks on curved stems springing from a central globe. Many were thrown out by nineteenth century restorers but a few remain. A delightful sixteenth century chandelier, probably German in origin, hangs in the south chapel of St John, Timberhill, Norwich and there is an eighteenth century example in Griston SS Peter and Paul.

Funerary Fashions, Brasses and Mural Monuments

From the twelfth century onwards the church became to a limited extent a mausoleum for the wealthy and influential and it remained so until the beginning of the nineteenth century. It has been argued that the lengthening of many a church chancel arose from the need to find room for the many who paid handsomely for the opportunity to have a burial place before or near the High Altar. There is no doubt that provision of a bone house or Carnary, duly sanctified and consecrated, became the only means whereby space could be found within the church for additional burials. At Rothwell, Northants is a carnery, an early thirteenth century room 30′ long and 15′ wide containing the bones of approximately 11,000 people. The carnery had been sealed at the time of the Reformation.

In Norfolk the earliest remaining funerary furniture are the few and widely scattered thirteenth century stone coffin lids, some decorated with enfoliated crosses and staffs. Of the same period or slightly later are the tomb chests, with or without effigies and these, for so populous a county as Norfolk, are scarce. At East Tuddenham is a thirteenth century knightly effigy holding a heart. Tombs of Sir Roger Kerdiston 1337 at Reepham and of Sir Oliver de Ingham 1344 at Ingham are strikingly similar. Both effigies recline in a twisted attitude on beds of pebbles, the reason for the attitude unknown. Then there are the late thirteenth Gerbrigge tombs and recesses at Wickhampton and an even more sumptuous recess without a tomb at Raveningham. Other than these the only other noteworthy funerary furnishings are the three oaken effigies at Banham, Fersfield and South Acre.

Absence of workable stone in the county may have accounted for the universal use of brasses towards the end of the thirteenth century. They remained fashionable for nearly five hundred years and Norfolk is rich in them from the small plate with an inscription beginning "Orate pro anima . . ." or "Hic jacet . . ." to the astoundingly rich Hastings brass in Elsing church, the Felbrigg and South Acre brasses and the grandiose Walsoken and Braunche brasses in King's Lynn St Margaret. Between these limits lie the wonderfully varied collection commemorating priests, merchants, laymen, squires and nobles. Many have disappeared leaving only their matrices to indicate vaguely their original wealth of detail. A few, known today as palimpsests, reveal that mediaeval robbery was no uncommon thing. These are memorial brasses torn from their original matrices, turned over and recut for another patron. In Reedham a brass inscribed to Alyce Yelverton is a palimpsest of another to Nicholas Lathe, a parchmyner. Early tomb chests, altar tombs and ledger slabs seldom bore inscriptions so we must conclude that the later engraver on brass was a tolerably literate fellow or a skilled copyist of the priest's Gothic script. By the sixteenth century brasses were no longer regularly set in the flooring to get worn by the passage of people's feet but were fixed instead to the sides of tombs or to the architectural treatments above these. And as Latin became frowned upon as a language of inscription, English supplanted it and a Latin script was used much inferior to the earlier Gothic.

Of the very few mediaeval tombs in alabaster the finest is undoubtedly that of Sir Edmund Thorpe and his wife in Aswellthorpe, early fifteenth century. It has been mentioned separately because it heralds the wide use of alabaster for mural monuments and standing monuments that began a fashion in the sixteenth century and continued through the following two hundred years. For a brief period after the Renaissance Italian influence brought in the use of terracotta for funerary monuments. Of these Norfolk has the sumptuous Bedingfeld tombs at Oxborough,

Ashwellthorpe All Saints. Effigies of Sir Edmund de Thorpe and wife, 1446. Both wear S.S. collars.

1525, the tomb of Abbot Ferrars at Wymondham, 1548, the Jannys tomb chest in Norwich St George Colegate and the outer frieze of an unknown tomb at Bracon Ash.

With the Reformation veneration of the Sacraments ceased, to be replaced by a peculiar veneration for the majesty of Death. Wealth once showered upon the church for masses to be sung for the souls of the donors was now bestowed upon production of mural monuments, frequently in alabaster and tricked out with macabre skulls and crossbones (see the Suckling tombs in Norwich St Andrews) or with ornamentation of burial tools (Stratton Strawless). This fashion lasted till the Restoration of 1660 when classical themes supplanted it and monuments and murals became decorated with cherub heads with wings and chubby little weeping putti. Standing or reclining effigies, often by the foremost sculptors of the day, reflected this classical slant, the ultimate being the ridiculous figure clad in classical armour and yet wearing a full bottomed wig (the Hare chapel in Stow Bardolph).

Hatchments

No more neglected a piece of church furniture exists than the hatchment, yet it is the outward expression of social custom from the seventeenth century almost to the twentieth.

A hatchment is a set of armorial bearings painted on canvas. The word is a corruption of "achievement", a heraldic term meaning "coat of arms". The frame is invariably rectangular, and hung diamond fashion on the wall. Thackeray called them "funeral compliments". They were hung and displayed outside the house of the deceased for a twelvemonth and then, parson's permission gained, were brought into the church and hung close to their appropriate vault or mural tablet.

Rules of heraldry applied in full to hatchments, in shield, mantling and crest. Backgrounds were distinguishing features. When a husband died, his arms, together with those of his wife, appeared impaled, that is, side by side. Background was divided "per pale", the deceased on the dexter (right) side being black, the sinister (left) side silver or white. If in either case the deceased were unmarried, the whole background was painted black. If the deceased were a spinster, then a lozenge instead of a shield bore her achievement.

Size of a hatchment indicates the period. Early examples are small and more carefully painted. Nineteenth century examples can be anything up to five feet across. A rococo style shield is early eighteenth century work. Spade shaped shields came in late in the same century.

Hoveton St John and St Peter retain hatchments of the Negus and Aufrere families, Worstead those of the Berneys and Brograves and Scottow those of the Durrants. These are but a few of the wealth of hatchments to be found in Norfolk churches.

Music of the Post Reformation Church and the Organ

Congregation participation began to assume a new importance in the seventeenth century although at first confined almost solely to the singing of metrical psalms and a chanting of the Psalms of the day from the Book of Common Prayer. Provision of tunes for metrical psalms was early provided by Thomas Sternhold, Henry VIII's Groom of the Wardrobe, and John Hopkins in 1551. Tunes were first given names in 1592. Together with Nahum Tate's tunes in 1696 these lasted until the nineteenth century when there occurred a spate of hymn tune composers. It became customary, during the singing of the first metrical psalm, for the parson to retire to his vestry to change from surplice to black gown in which he preached his hour long sermon. Then followed the second psalm.

Pitch of the tunes was decided with the aid of a pitch pipe. It was a wooden pipe with a graduated plunger rather like a square sectioned bicycle pump. You pushed in the plunger to the graduation marking the required note and blew.

With increased congregation participation the pitch pipe was gradually superseded by the church band. Anyone who could play an instrument took part. Favoured instruments were the violin, 'cello, bass viol, clarinet and serpent. Canon K. H. Macdermott in his *Old Church Gallery Minstrels* (S.P.C.K. London, 1948) lists 266 church orchestras between 1660 and 1860. This can be but a fraction of all the church bands of the past.

The Gothic revival created violent changes in the music of the parish church. The clergy began to envy the cathedrals with their surpliced choirs and their pipe organs. The sturdy independence of the old church bands — with their occasional mistakes and misdemeanours — and their co-partners the singing galleries — see Hogarth's picture of an eighteenth century choir — led to their unpopularity with the clergy. Many only awaited the slightest excuse to get rid of their unwelcome assistants. So they went and with them went the seventeenth century chancel box pews to make way for a set of choir stalls and a surpliced choir.

The popular accompaniment of a choir was the pipe organ. There had been organs in the past. In the tenth century an organ at Winchester required two men to play the instrument and twenty eight men to blow the bellows while "the roaring thereof could be heard throughout the city". In mediaeval times the monasteries and cathedrals had their great and their portative organs. But not until the late seventeenth century did the organ come to find a place in the larger and more wealthy parish churches. Difficulty of finding enough people capable of performing upon the instrument limited their wider use. An expedient had to be found and, in consequence, a German invention, the barrel organ, came to be installed in many a parish church. The first was in 1700 and by 1879 there were known more than 500 in English churches. The late Canon Noel Boston located 35 in Norfolk alone. Some had been converted to finger organs, a few to complete

Gooderstone: typical example of a chamber organ ⟡
put to church use during the nineteenth century.

but small manual organs. Today only six can be said to be in workable condition as barrel organs. They are at West Bradenham, Bressingham, Letheringsett, Mattishall Burgh, North Lopham, Witton and Wood Rising. Only at Mattishall Burgh and Wood Rising are they still in use in their original form.

Most finger organs have by now been converted to manual instruments. The county possesses many a fine organ made by some of the best nineteenth century organ builders in the country. Some dainty little instruments, encased most charmingly, have come from private houses. Those at Blickling, Easton, Fersfield and Wickhampton are examples of such a change of environment.

There are four organs by Snetzler, Blickling, 1762, St Margaret, King's Lynn, 1754 (constructed to the order of Dr Burney who in it introduced the dulciana stop to England) Hillington and Sculthorpe.

Bells and Bell Casting

Discovery of a bell casting pit beneath the foundations of a Saxon church recently uncovered from beneath the earthworks of Castle Rising castle could probably explain why bells have been regarded from early times with peculiar sanctity.

Bell casting — or founding — was in all likelihood an ecclesiastical "mystery" performed in the secrecy of a part finished church and accompanied by appropriate prayers, the ritual repetition of which was the only way whereby the process could be correctly timed. The finished article was probably ready to sound its message and call the faithful to worship by the time the building was completed.

According to archaeological experts responsible for the work at Castle Rising, the method of casting used was the traditional one employing wax. A pit was dug and lined with large stones sufficient to support the weight of the core, or centre mould, together with the bell metal. Within this was erected the cope, a mould shaping the bell. Materials used for this purpose are still traditional, clay mixed with manure and hair. The mixture sets hard and successive coats are spread on the cope and dried off to get a perfect surface which will take a burnish. This ensures the smoothness of the outer surface of the bell. When finished, the cope was plastered with wax which could be scraped to the correct thickness of the bell about to be cast. Finally the whole was filled with the core made of the same materials as that of the cope. The process must have taken many days. Finally heat was applied to melt the wax and molten bell metal poured into the cavity.

Everything now had to dry out slowly under gentle heat for neither core nor cope must be allowed to crack.

How early Saxon bells were hung and rung remains a mystery. These ancient bells were certainly large and most certainly rung because pre-Conquest England was known as the "Ringing Island". Bells were thought to possess mystical qualities. For example, the deep tones of St Guthlac of Crowland Abbey in the Fens were said to cure the headache and could be heard for miles.

Bells were considered aids to devotion. The Mass Bell summoned all to worship in the early morning, the Gabriel Bell was rung at the saying or singing of the Ave Maria, the Sanctus during every sacrament of the Mass so that those in the fields could pause and pray at the elevation of the Host. The Vesper Bell, later to be known as the Curfew, originally signalled Evensong and continued until the Reformation. As a warning against the possibility of fire the practice was continued and carried on well into this century as for example at St Giles, Norwich.

No very early bell survives. The crystalline character of bell metal is one factor that makes necessary occasional recasting. Accident, use and general neglect are additionally no aids to longevity in bells. By Royal decree many were removed at the Reformation. Sequestrators were ordered to leave only one bell and that usually the smallest. Of the four earliest remaining bells in the country, thirteenth century and inscribed in Gothic capitals, one is in Norfolk at Deopham St Andrew.

As far as we know Saxon bells carried no inscription. That on a mediaeval bell usually took the form of a prayer. "Sit nomen Domini Benedictum" and "Ave Maria Gratia Plena Domini Tecum" are two of the more common prayers.

The earliest treatise on bell founding is by Walter de Odyngton, a monk of Evesham Abbey living in the mid-thirteenth century. It consists of only twelve lines of Latin and confirms what has already been said about the method used in Saxon times.

In the late fourteenth century the mystery of bell founding escaped from ecclesiastical into secular hands. It has been suggested that William de Belyetene of Canterbury was, in 1325 the first known bell founder. Records also mention John Langhorne of London, 1379-1405 but Thomas Potter of Norwich runs him pretty close and we know he gained his freedom in 1404. He was followed by Richard Brasyer, who worked in Potter's foundry. He died in 1482 and was succeeded by his son Richard who continued the business until 1513. Some of the Brasyers' bells, still in existence in the county, bear the city's arms.

Introduction of change ringing in the eighteenth century led to the disappearance of many an ancient bell. Demand was now for a ring of bells accurate in tone and of lighter weight. Great bells had no place in the new system and their retention could only be for the purpose of chiming, like Big Ben of Whitehall and Great Tom of St Pauls.

Norwich St John Maddermarket. Note the octagonal North porch, three-light Perpendicular clerestory windows, flushwork on tower buttresses and processional way beneath the tower.

CHAPTER EIGHT

Norwich Churches

There are 32 remaining mediaeval churches within the walls of the ancient city. At no time is the visitor out of sight of one or more of them. In a distance of less than one mile from St Benedict's gates to the Cathedral he passes St Benedict (now only the tower left) St Swithin, St Margaret, St Gregory, St Lawrence, St John Maddermarket, St Andrew, St Peter Hungate and St George Tombland. Modern building development may dwarf them individually but it cannot hide their presence or mask their mediaeval charm.

Alas, Norwich has too many churches. It is a tragic but outstanding fact of today that there they stand sentinel over an ancient parish system and with no parishioners to fill the pews. Perhaps there have always been too many and that only in times when piety and religious feeling were dominant were they ever partially filled. It is significant that, throughout the centuries there has always been a mortality. Many disappeared in mediaeval days while in this century St Edmund, St Swithin and St Mary the Less have been put to secular uses and St Peter Hungate has become an ecclesiastical museum. Of the four victims of wartime bombing, St Benedict, St Paul, St Michael at Thorn and St Julian, only the last has been rebuilt.

In recent years economic, social and living conditions have undergone drastic change and the Church now maintains that it cannot afford to keep in repair churches that have lost all their parishioners and worshippers and whose only value appears to be that of museum pieces. Happily Norwich City Council, encouraged in its action by the Norwich Society and the Society for the Preservation of Norwich Churches, has acknowledged its duty to preserve intact this wonderful heritage of mediaeval buildings, probably the finest civic collection in Europe. So, at least for this generation, the 32 churches and their churchyards within the walls of the city are safe from the envious eyes of property speculators.

At the time this passage was being revised news was given that the Queen had confirmed an order that the freehold of 6 of the 16 redundant churches were to be given to the City Council. These were immediately handed over to the Norwich Historic Churches Trust which acts as managers for the property. It is good to know that plans for their secular use have already been implemented. One becomes a costume museum, another a training school for stone masons, a third an exhibition centre and a fourth a community centre.

There is always a possibility that, should population again flow back to take its rightful place within the old boundaries, and if devotional practice revives, that the city's heritage of churches may yet experience a return to their first and consecrated purpose, perhaps more bountifully than at any time in their existence.

There is no Georgian church in Norwich: all are mediaeval, and the majority, with minor differences, are Perpendicular. This means that most were erected, or rebuilt on earlier foundations, when the city's prosperity was at its peak. Slight similarities abound, such as flushwork patterns of shields and lozenges in tower parapets, porches continuing the aisles rather than being in front of them — probably occasioned by lack of space — two-storeyed porches, vaulted porches and porches with figures in relief in the spandrels. What Georgian work there is can be seen in the handsome woodwork of pew, pulpit and reredos in those churches once favoured by eighteenth century wealth and industry and in the two Nonconformist meeting houses in Colegate, the Octagon Chapel and the Old Meeting House.

All Saints, All Saints Green

The early unbuttressed west tower has a Perpendicular top. Fenestration of the nave is Perpendicular and of the chancel Decorated. The porch is plain and one storeyed. Inside, the three bay arcade has octagonal piers and four centred arches. The fifteenth century font is exceptionally good, one of the two best in Norwich (q. v. St James) Against the faces of the octagonal bowl are eight standing figures of apostles and evangelists, there is a lovely enfoliated trail to the corona and the shaft has eight standing figures under canopied niches whose mould is linked with the trail. The church kept its box pews until 1929.

Monuments, as in all the city churches, commemorate past merchants and important city functionaries and ancient parish charities are remembered either by memorials to the donors or on separate boards.

St Andrew, Broad Street

The earlier church was probably erected on the first piece of high ground above the water meadows, so today this completely Perpendicular church stands high above the street. Its west tower was built first in 1478 as can be seen by the north and south porches which embrace it and in which are the base course which was originally meant to be seen from outside. The rest was built in 1506 according to the inscription of 1547 on the west wall of the south aisle. Only a frieze of shields below the east window is older, the heraldry of which is puzzling for it includes arms of The Holy Roman Empire, England (1340-1405), Bishop Despenser, Earl of Arundel and the city arms as well as the usual ecclesiastical symbols of the Blessed Sacrament and Instruments of the Passion.

The interior is almost as big as that of St Peter Mancroft, in fact a typical hall church where the slender piers of the five bay arcades with their four centred arches never seem an obstruction. Aisles extend east from the porches to within one bay of the east end. Above the arcades is blank tracery and over all a great range of clerestory three-light windows. The roof is a cambered tie-beam. The aisles have the outer walls arcaded and modern roofs. Both porches have parvises and central, stooled and canopied niches with windows each side.

Much of the furnishing is in the best tradition of Victorian work and this includes the font, the pulpit, the low screen of 1870, the reredos of 1856 and the organ case of 1908. The font cover is dated 1637 and consists of four columns, an open-work obelisk in the middle, an octagonal canopy with a ball at the top.

There is good fifteenth glass in the south aisle windows, some containing heraldic shields, others showing iconographic subjects, Death and the Bishop, angels worshipping the Virgin and Isaac ascending the Mount. The church is rich in brasses and monuments, two of which are by Rawlins, a well-known sculptor of the eighteenth century. In the Suckling chapel are monuments to Robert (Mayor in 1572 and 1872) and his son John who died in 1613, also to Francis Rugge (Mayor in 1587, 1598 and 1602) and to Robert Garsett, 1613. The largest is to Sir John Suckling and his wife, a wonderful alabaster work where he lies in armour, reclining by his wife. Symbols of mortality in the form of skulls and bones are prominent and beneath the funerary slab, difficult to see, is an emaciated figure in a shroud.

Sword and mace rests are unusual in that the names of the six Mayors mentioned are given in Latin. The organ by Norman and Beard, case designed by H. F. Green.

St Augustine

A large church with a stately west tower of brick built in 1726 but incorporating earlier sound holes. There are north and south aisles, chancel aisles and a projecting south porch. The tower has clasping buttresses and a battlemented parapet. The chancel is as long as the nave and has a steep tiled roof descending to the aisles. Because of its height the nave appears shorter than the chancel, has a low-pitched lead roof and a clerestory of wide spaced Perpendicular windows (three-light). The roof is arch braced with camber tie beams and there are arch braces between the wall posts. The principals are 15' apart and there is no purlin or collar.

The plain fifteenth century octagonal font has a traceried bowl and little engaged columns around the shaft. A single panel of the old screen remains showing St Appolonia with her pincers.

At the west end the tall tower arch has a ringing chamber in its upper half railed off with Georgian balusters that were originally altar rails.

Among the memorials mention must be made of that of Matthew Brettingham, a large tablet in the vestry. He was architect of several great Norfolk houses including Holkham, Gunton and Langley.

The church owns a New Testament of Edward VI in Latin and English with a Paraphrase or commentary by Erasmus. The only other I know is at Mattishall.

St Benedict

Only the round tower remains with its polygonal top stage. The church was bombed in 1942.

St Andrew's Hall and its Chancel, Blackfriars Hall

These are included here because fundamentally they are a church though today used for secular purposes. It was the church of the Blackfriars (Dominicans) from 1307 until its dissolution in 1536. It is a unique example of a preaching church. The fabric was well restored in 1863 by T. D. Barry, the city surveyor and to him are due the west wall and the west doorway, the south porch and the arch at the east end of the nave.

The church is entirely Perpendicular but for the south aisle windows and the great east window of seven-lights. The clerestory has twice the number of lights — fourteen — as the bays inside. The arcades are tall and have piers of four shafts with four shallow concave curves in the diagonals. The arches are two-centred.

The only remaining monument is that to John Ellison, 1639 who was pastor of the Dutch congregation.

Remains of the cloister are approached from the north aisle. The walks are buttressed and vaulted and there is an upper storey. The arches are of brick and quadruple chamfered. The east wall only of the east range remains and between that and the chancel is an undercroft known as Becket's Chapel. It has a stone pier in the middle and brick vaulting. Recent excavation (summer, 1974) has uncovered foundations of further sections of the cloisters.

St Clement, Colegate

The complete dedication is to St Clement the Martyr, unusual in East Anglia. The church is claimed by some writers to be the oldest in the city. It has a slender Perpendicular west tower and against the parapet, in flushwork, shields in lozenges. Nave and chancel are Perpendicular except for the Decorated east window. There are no aisles, the span being over 29', and no porches, only small doors north and south each with a window above. A little vestry to the north makes one facade different from the other. The white tomb chest on the south graveyard is a nineteenth century rebuild of the tomb erected to his parents by Matthew Parker, Archbishop of Canterbury under Queen Elizabeth.

The interior is short and wide, the chancel much lower and narrower. The tower arch is tall. The chancel roof is arch braced, carried on wall posts which have longitudinal arch braces and are decorated with angels. The font, octagonal, has fleurons on the stem and flowers and leaves on the bowl. On the floor of the nave is a brass to Margaret Pettwode, 1514.

The furnishings are all Victorian and date from the restoration of 1889 when the west gallery was removed. The walls carry memorial tablets to the Ives and Harvey families.

St Edmund, Fishergate

Disused and for many years a factory store standing on but a remnant of its graveyard, its north side close to the street. The tower is Perpendicular with a traceried west sound hole. There is a south aisle and a south chapel. The nave and chancel are under one roof and the porch and vestry are on the north side. The arcade has four-centred arches peculiarly arranged, two bays, a small window-like opening, a third bay with foliated little caps, another opening and finally the two bay chapel. Nave, chancel and wide aisle are well lit with large Perpendicular windows.

The church was stripped of its Georgian furnishings in 1882. It is reported that in the middle ages the church possessed a piece of the shirt of St Edward, King and Martyr, kept in a box of crystal.

St Etheldreda, King Street

This would be a foundation of the late Saxon settlement, probably after the Danish invasion and situated in the oldest street in the city. Two churchyards are close to where the city walls descend towards the river. In one are the few remains of St Peter Southgate and in the other is St Etheldreda. This too is in a parlous state and has been closed since 1961, its windows boarded up, its one bell stolen.

The low round tower has an octagonal top with a brick trim. The nave is aisleless, there is a south Saxo-Norman doorway much restored but with one cap in a good state of preservation. On both south and north walls are lengths of zigzag string course. The font has shields on the bowl faces and small heads on the corona.

Monuments are from St Peter Southgate:- William Johnson, 1611, with groups of figures in relief kneeling and facing each other and framed with tapering pilasters: John Paul, 1726, a tablet with books in a prie-dieu.

St George, Colegate

A church that still shows evidence of the eighteenth century wealth from weaving that surrounded it. It stands at the crossing of Colegate and St George Street — once known as Gildengate because it led to the Gildencroft. Of its building several dates are recorded; nave and tower 1459, the chancel about 1498, in 1505 the north aisle was added and in 1513 the south aisle.

The tower is tall, diagonally buttressed, with square traceried sound holes, tall three-light bell openings, battlements with flushwork decoration and shields in lozenges. There is a decayed west doorway with remains of flushwork panelling to left and right and a frieze of shields above. Fenestration is all late Perpendicular and the clerestory is ashlar faced. The nave has a tall but low pitched roof and that of the chancel is lower. A two-storeyed porch is attached to the south aisle. Inside one steps into what is practically a Georgian interior because much of its furnishings have at some time or other been removed from other Norwich churches. At the west end one passes between columns supporting a classical gallery on which now stands the charming little organ built by George Pope England, 1802 and restored to almost original condition. The case is early eighteenth century work. The pews are late eighteenth and early nineteenth century work. The reredos is Georgian and the magnificent pulpit with back board and tester is eighteenth century. One panel only is decorated with inlaid mosaic work in wood of various colours depicting flowers and foliage.

The three bay arcades have piers of four shafts — four hollows section — and four centred arches. On the south aisle are wall arches. Between the six close-set clerestory windows are the wall posts which rest on angels and are joined by longitudinal arch braces. The roof is of cambered tie beams on arched braces.

The font is thirteenth century of Purbeck marble style with two shallow arches to each face, but the material is not Purbeck marble. There are three sets of sword and mace rests.

The church is rich in monuments, the earliest being a brass to William Norwiche and wife, 1468 (north chapel). The earliest tomb is that of Robert Jannys (Mayor 1517 and 1524) in terracotta and probably the work of the same artists who made the Oxborough and Wymondham tombs. Another tomb chest has baluster pilasters and decorated panels. Two small putti left and right flank an inscription between pilasters to Thomas Hall, 1715. A standing monument with a semi-reclining cherub commemorates Thomas Pinder Sen. 1722, by Robert Singleton. That to Timothy Balderston, 1764, is by Thomas Rawlins — a putto on a curvaceous sarchophagus holding an inscribed parchment. In the south aisle is a memorial to John Crome the painter who lived in the parish.

A few vestiges of fourteenth century mural painting remain around the moulding of the west window of the north aisle and there is a conservation cross on the north wall.

The churches of St Margaret at Colegate and St Olave were taken down and their parishes combined with St George's, the former in 1349, the latter in 1546.

St George, Tombland

Enclosed on north and west sides by Tombland Alley its west tower is 1445 but it underwent repair in 1645. Below the west window is a niche and there are traceried sound holes. The flushwork parapet carries big lozenges and shields. The north porch, sixteenth century is attached to the aisle. It has a canopied double niche over the entrance.

Both north and south porches are vaulted and have a parvise. The south porch has a tierceron star vault and a centre boss of St George and the Dragon. It has a parapet with flushwork quatrefoils. The north porch, now used as a chapel, has simple chamfered ribs. The clerestory is continuous through nave and chancel.

The five bay nave arcades are fourteenth century, octagonal piers with triple chamfered arches. The chancel arch is of the same period but a north chapel of one bay has a four centred arch with an octagonal respond on the west only. The high tower arch is fifteenth century with slim attached shafts.

The font is thirteenth century, hexagonal, of Purbeck marble, on a main shaft with four Purbeck marble colonettes. It is panelled with two shallow arches on each face. The font cover is Jacobean — supported by eight columns with an open work obelisk in the centre and a statuette of St George surmounting all. The fine panelled pulpit with back board and tester is seventeenth century.

Most of the glass is late Victorian but in a high nave window are two roundels of what look like Flemish sixteenth century glass. The reredos is typical eighteenth century work with a broken pediment on Corinthian columns. Furnishings include the Royal Arms of Anne, an iron bound chest, mace and sword stands, an oak plaque, early sixteenth century probably German, with original colouring, depicting the story of St George in relief. What is probably a dole table in marble lies beneath the tomb of Sir John Symonds, 1609.

Monuments, of which there are many, include one by Nicholas Stone erected to Alderman Anguish, 1617, (now part hidden by the organ) kneeling figures facing over a prayer desk; one to May Gardner, 1748 and to Thomas Maltby, 1760. Both these last have cherubs as themes. In accordance with present day High Anglican practice, this church is beautifully cared for.

St Giles

A church in the New Burgh, it was founded soon after the Norman Conquest by Elwyn the priest who gave the living to the Great Monastery of Norwich. Consequently it is now in the patronage of the Dean and Chapter. The church was rebuilt in the reign of Richard II but the chancel was demolished — for economy's sake — in 1581 — and not rebuilt until the nineteenth century.

St Giles stands on the north side of the street on one of the highest points in the city, a fact that enhances the height of its already 120' tall tower. It was a beacon tower and the iron basket which held the fire is still preserved in the church. The buttresses are in-line, ending with a deep set-off at the foot of the last stage. Above that they appear as thin clasping pilasters. Parapet and buttresses are decorated with flushwork and the tower is finished with a pretty cupola, 1737. The bell openings are tall four-lights with transoms and in the middle stage are three-light blanks with transoms. There is a Perpendicular west window and below it a Perpendicular west doorway.

The church was built in the early fifteenth century but the Victorian Decorated chancel by Phipson can bear but little relation to the original. The south porch is ashlar faced, has a top frieze with shields in running tendrils a handsome cresting and a fan vault — the only one in the city — which puts the porch as at least fifty years after the rest of the church. There are stooled and canopied niches flanking the three-light parvise window.

Inside are arcades of five bays. The piers have four shafts, capped, with multiple moulding between which is carried over the four centred arches. The chancel arch corresponds to this and is flanked with three tiers of canopied niches.

The hammer beam roof is an early example of such work. Bosses support the hammer beam and the braces rising on it are constructed in one unbroken curve from the wall posts to the top without collar beams. Angels on the hammer beams cut across the braces and finish at the wall posts.

The font has little faces on the underside and flowers and little shields around the bowl.

Furnishings include five sword and mace rests and the benches are Victorian and of fine workmanship. The glass of the east window was given by Sir Peter Eade in 1904. The many monuments are a fine collection. That to Alderman Thomas Churchman, 1742 is by Sir Henry Cheere and there are two by Thomas Rawlins — Philip Stannard, 1747 and Sir Thomas Churchman, 1781.

Brasses in the nave floor commemorate Robert Baxter, Mayor 1424 and Richard Purdance, 1436. In the south aisle is a chalice brass to John Smythe, 1499.

The organ is by Hill and built originally as a practice organ for Dr Zachariah Buck, 1866. Its new chancel and west front cases are by Ralph Bootman, 1966-7.

St Gregory

Another of the churches whose Saxon foundation was laid upon the high ground immediately above the Wensum water meadows and flood plain. This can

Norwich St Gregory. The sanctuary knocker.

Norwich St Gregory. The clerestory is decorated, the tower contains some Saxon work.

be said of all the churches along St Benedict's Street and all have early dedications. The tower contains an interior Saxon splay. By the time the present church was built the area was hedged in to east and west so its chancel was raised to provide a processional way beneath. There is a small crypt.

The west tower is tall with flushwork battlements. Its spire, the only one in the city other than that of the Cathedral, was destroyed in 1840. The west door-way, which has panelling up one moulding of the jambs, is inside a small Galilee porch with quadripartite vaulting. The bell openings are Decorated north and south porches, both two storeyed, are attached to the west walls of the aisles and flank the tower. The south porch has two bays of quadripartite vaulting with ridge fibs and bosses. Over the entrance is a pinnacled niche and above that a clock in a pedimented frame with architrave and fluted pillars.

The interior of the tower is interesting. It is tierceron vaulted and above that is a stone gallery, its underside also vaulted. Under the tower is a traceried stoup. Close by is the font, octagonal, its bowl with shields, its shaft panelled. The corona has eight angels who gaze down upon eight grotesque heads crushed to represent carnal desires destroyed by baptism. The cover is Jacobean.

The four-bay arcade is intermediate Decorated/Perpendicular, the piers with four sturdy shafts and thin shafts in the diagonals, castellated polygonal caps, and two-centred arches. The eight close set clerestory two-light windows are in keeping with these. The aisle walls are arcaded, the piers projecting 16″ with the re-entrant angles rounded. Aisle windows are Perpendicular.

The chancel which projects one bay east of the arcades was rebuilt 1394 at the charge of the Cathedral Priory.

Only three panels of the screen survive portraying St John the Baptist and Barbara, the third an angel. Of the mediaeval furnishings are four stalls in the chancel with misericords bearing carvings of a bearded man, two angels and a lion. The lectern is one of the famous fifteenth century East Anglian variety. The Sanctuary Knocker, fourteenth century, similar to one in Durham Cathedral is now in Norwich Castle Museum. The boss is a lion's head with a man's head in its jaws. On the west wall of the north aisle is a Mural of St George, restored in 1861. In the background the church is depicted with its spire. The church was the head-quarters of the Guild of St George which, being esteemed part of the City Cor-poration, was not dissolved by Edward VI.

A few pieces of fifteenth century glass are in a north aisle window. The church possesses a sixteenth century pall depicting dolphins in gold thread with fish half eaten in their mouths. It symbolises the Greek IXOUS — a fish — emblem of "Jesu Christou Theou Uios Soter," "Jesus Christ Son of God our Saviour". Given by John Read and Maud his wife. A portion of a sixteenth century crimson velvet cope made into an altar cloth and inscribed, "Pray for the souls of John Westgate and Agnes his wife."

Monuments include, 1659, Francis Bacon, a big tomb chest in the south aisle bearing reputedly the longest epitaph in England. 1668, Sir Joseph Payne, 1715, Sir Peter Seaman (by Thomas Green of Camberwell), 1762, Joseph Chamberlin (by Thomas Ivory).

St Helen

A church within a church, the secular infirmary enclosing the parochial. The Great Hospital was founded by Bishop Walter de Suffield in 1249 as a hospital for aged priests and poor people. Despite drastic changes made in the late Tudor period the original plan is still clear — a long aisled infirmary hall with an aisleless chancel, typical of mediaeval monastic infirmaries.

Of the building as seen today, in point of time, the south tower and the porch come first. The tower, for which money was left in 1374, projects west from the west wall. The porch, Limbert's Porch, could be the original. It is three bays long with single chamfered vaulting ribs, conceivably thirteenth century. Its parvise was repaired in 1754. The porch connects with the east end of the nave which is the parish church. Chancel and west end of the nave are walled off and remain wards of the Great Hospital, of which see below.

The three bays have the usual, apparently late fourteenth century quatrefoil piers, thin polygonal shafts in the diagonals and polygonal caps all of which could have been accepted by Bishop Goldwell in his 1480 rebuild.

The south transept chapel has a sumptuous lierne vaulted roof, bosses depicting the Assumption, the Annunciation, the Nativity, Ascension and Resurrection, secular scenes connected with Christ's infancy as well as SS Catherine, Edward, Edmund, Margaret and the twelve Apostles. There are 16 bench ends with poppyheads, those on the front being very good, one of Margaret of Antioch and the Dragon with "hec" underneath for Hecker (Master of the Hospital 1519-22). Other furnishings are delightfully eighteenth century, box pews and a raised pulpit at the east end, the "Ivory" pew, in Gothic style in the transept inscribed to William and Thomas Ivory, an organ case of the same period together with Georgian hymn boards and splendidly lettered and coloured Creed and Commandment Boards as reredos behind a fine early Stuart table. Additional are eighteenth century sword and mace rests.

Two mediaeval features are, one, a miniature three-light Perpendicular window overlooking the church from the walled-in porch bay, the other a banner stave locker beside the north door from the cloisters.

Of the infirmary section of the building — divided vertically into wards in the

Norwich St Helen. Wooden roof boss on the Eagle roof of the chancel.

Norwich St Helen. The Eagle roof of the chancel, said to have been designed to commemorate the visit of Anne of Bohemia.

mid seventeenth century — mention here need only be made of the chancel roof and of some of the fenestration. The ceiling of the chancel is a half dodecagon in section and has panels filled with 252 spread-winged black eagles (in honour of Anne of Bohemia, wife of Richard II) and many bosses with enfoliated heads. The seven-light east window is early Perpendicular and the north chancel windows alternate between Perpendicular and Decorated.

St James, Pockthorpe.

The church is now used as a night hostel for the homeless. It is mainly Perpendicular though parts appear to be older. Considerable restoration was done in 1842 and 1882. The church consists of a chancel and vestry, a nave, south aisle, south porch and west tower. The west end is of peculiar design, tripartite inside, the middle section supporting and embracing the tower on east, south and north arches. The tower has an octagonal brick top showing all headers and embattled. The south porch is joined to the south aisle and has little seated figures as pinnacles. The nave roof sweeps down to cover the south aisle. The three bay nave/arcade has two additional bays in the chancel all with octagonal piers and four centred arches.

The charming fourteenth century font has eight standing stooled figures of female saints under vaulted canopies around the shaft. The corona has a lovely trail of interlaced tree branches rising from the shaft's engaged colonettes with entwined foliage. On each of the bowl's faces are two standing figures of saints with emblems.

There are a number of sixteenth century Flemish glass panels in the windows and two fifteenth century Norwich heads.

The modern screen incorporates some painted panels from a former screen which were restored to the church in 1917 by Russell Colman. They had been cast out during the restoration and had been offered for sale on the market place at a shilling each.

St John, Maddermarket

Maddermarket takes its name from madder, a dye sold when weaving was the city's staple industry. The church consists of a nave of three bays with aisles and chapels, north and south porches and an embattled tower under which is an arched north/south pathway. Above the stone faced parapet are the four Evangelists as pinnacles. Though no documentary evidence exists it is thought there was once a chancel, probably raised high upon steps and spanning a right of way similar to that at St Gregory. Lack of space for processional purposes often made this arrangement a necessity. The church is mainly Perpendicular but the east window is Decorated a fact that makes the chancel theory difficult to accept unless the window was later reset.

The tower is richly decorated with flint panelling on the buttresses in white stone. The bell openings are three-light and the sound holes are square and traceried. The clerestory has eight three-light windows closely set and faced with ashlar. Both porches are two-storeyed, that on the north semi-octagonal with buttresses. The south porch has a damaged vault, the north a tierceron star vault with an additional circular rib connecting the bosses. The north entrance has two sets of suspended shields in the casement moulding of jambs and arch, and above is a three-light window under a square label surmounting a niche.

The interior has three bay arcades of slim Perpendicular piers with thin shafts and wave mouldings in the diagonals. In the north aisle wall are wall arches. At the west end the church is darkened by a gallery overhead and closed from the rest of the nave with a twentieth century gated screen. At the east end is a sumptuous eighteenth century baldachino with panelled back flanked with engaged fluted balusters with Corinthian caps. The handsome tester has a classical trail in place of entablature and above the cornice is a broken pediment. Support for this is again two fluted columns with Corinthian caps. Although the Communion rails and lectern are twentieth century they are harmonious. A little north chapel is enclosed with screens, the one Gothic, the other Jacobean.

In the south aisle are monuments to the Layers and Sothertons, sixteenth century Mayors of the city. On the north wall a tablet commemorates Lady Margaret, Duchess of Norfolk. As she died under a political cloud, her husband having been beheaded, she was buried at midnight. Despite this drawback, description of her funeral cortege reads like a page from Scott's *Kenilworth*. The tablet was not erected until 1791.

The church has a rich collection of civic brasses, now on the west wall and difficult to see under the gallery. They date from 1412 to 1608 and at least two are palimpsests. That of Robert Rugge, 1558, Alderman and twice Mayor, has effigies of himself in civic gown, Elizabeth his wife and four sons, with shields, scrolls and an inscription. This brass is a palimpsest of a fourteenth century abbot.

There are fragments of ancient glass in some of the windows and the east window contains good Victorian glass.

The organ is by Robert Hope-Jones, 1897. It is the only Hope-Jones organ left in the city and one of the very few in the country. This is not in a good condition.

St John, Timberhill

South porch, nave, north and south aisles and chancel chapels. Though dated 1837 the porch incorporates much mediaeval work including vaulting and parvise. Yet originally the entrance most used was north-east, now the vestry door. This church was an early foundation and there is a portion of Saxon long-and-short work in the east wall, probably a demarcation of the early dimensions. The tower collapsed in 1784. Except for the east window all is Perpendicular. The three bay arcades have the usual quatrefoil piers with octagonal caps and three chamfered arches. North responds are semicircular, south responds polygonal. The modern barrel roof is lit by two dormers. There is an original door to the parvise and remains of a priest's door below a window on the south.

The font is plain, the cover modern and well conceived. The chancel screen is said to have come from Horstead church in the 1890s. Above is a modern rood loft and a rood with figures from Oberammergau.

The south chapel too is screened and lit by a lovely chandelier built around a figure of the Virgin amid foliage of vine leaves (said by Pevsner to be of German origin), c. 1500. The chapel reredos, a triptych is lit by another candelabrum, c. 1700.

Of monuments one of Norwich's best is on the chancel wall where a putto mourns the death of Robert Page, 1778, the city's most famous funerary sculptor.

Sword and mace rests, near the south door contain names of John Angell, Mayor 1830, and Arthur Michael Samuel, Lord Mayor, 1912-13, writer and politician who was born in the parish.

St John de Sepulchre

Until 1099 the dedication of this ancient Saxon foundation was John the Baptist. The church stands on the highest point above the river in what must have been the earliest settlement there. Today its tower dominates the southern skyline of the city. The dedication was changed when the Holy Sepulchre was captured from the Saracens. The present building consists of west tower, nave, north and south transepts and chancel. The nave has pillars and four centred arches along the walls giving the impression of there once having been aisles. The tower, fifteenth century, of four stages has two light Perpendicular bell openings, traceried sound holes, panelled diagonal buttresses and a panelled parapet with shields and four crocketed pinnacles, the last being added in 1904. The north porch is groined with a parvise over and a tall stooled and canopied niche between two windows. Below, a frieze of shields and one of flushwork divide the storeys. The vault is simple tierceron and the north door itself is pleasingly traceried.

The church was subjected to major restoration in 1866 resulting in modern furnishings. In 1914 was added a rather gawdy figured reredos designed by John Oldrid Scott. The screen is a puzzle and could be a mixture of parts old and not so old. Painted figures in the panels are dim with varnish and yet bear the stamp of nineteenth century about them.

There is also a doubtful consecration cross again over-painted and varnished. The Nave roof is arch braced but I do not think it has other than mediaeval parts in it.

The font is East Anglian, octagonal, its faces bearing lions alternating with two angels and two arch angels. At the base diagonals are seated lions between gabled pilasters. Winged heads look down from the corona. Monuments include a tablet to Bernard Church, a staunch Roundhead and Mayor, 1651, and a large wall tablet to one James Watts, a butcher. There are brasses to a civilian and his wife, 1530, one of which is a palimpsest of a monk under a canopy behind a grille.

St Julian

Once the most Saxon of city churches on the south ridge above the river. After being bombed the building has been extensively rebuilt. The dedication is is supposedly Julian the Hospitaller, patron saint of travellers. Of the round tower only a stump remains. In the north wall are two occuli with deep double splays. One other window is similar but arched. In the original church these were quoined only with flint. There was also a plinth round the lower part of the walls. In the tower are remains of circular but blocked openings.

On the south side, in place of the once existent cell of the anchoress Juliana of Norwich, has been built a memorial chapel. Its entrance, Saxo-Norman, comes from the bombed church of St Michael at Thorn in Ber Street. It has one order of shafts and single scallop caps and the arch has two zig-zag mouldings with twisted rope between.

The fifteenth century font is octagonal, has a panelled shaft and angels with shields around the bowl.

St Lawrence

One of the great hall churches of the city dated 1472, without a chancel arch and which partially fits into the plan of St Peter Mancroft, Andrew and Stephen. The west tower is 112′ high, flushwork panelled two step battlements and the north-east stair turret rising above them and topped with a spiret. The bell openings are Decorated and there is a good flushwork base course with shields in quatrefoils. The great west window has a casement mould with stools for figures. Below this a band of tracery, the stonework much deteriorated, separates window from west door in the spandrels of which are, left, the martyrdom of St Lawrence, right, that of St Edmund.

The north porch has a lierne vault and its outer door is dated 1663. The south porch has a niche, once stooled, with parvise lights left and right. The south entrance door is richly traceried.

The aisles have four-light windows, the clerestory eleven, closely set. The east window is Victorian Perpendicular 1894.

The three bay arcades lengthen eastwards to the two bay chancel chapels. The nave piers are octagonal with rounded angles, the chapel piers have a normal Perpendicular section of four shafts but only those towards the arches capped. Both aisle and chapel windows are set in wall arches. The roof is a magnificent hammer beam with long wall posts and arch braced and longitudinally braced. The whole rests on angel corbels. The fifteenth century font is unusual. It stands on a base with fleurons, has a short shaft panelled with quatrefoils in two tiers, a corona of supporting heads and an octagonal bowl the faces filled with shields held up by angels whose heads rise above each frame. The rim is castellated.

The chancel rises ten steps to accommodate a crypt. Furnishings are late nineteenth and early twentieth century. Memorials include a brass to Geffrey Langley, 1436, Prior of Horsham St Faiths (north side the nave) a skeleton brass, 1452 (south side) of a priest named Thomas Childes. In the nave floor John Asger, Sen. 1436, John Asger, Jun. 1436 and John Stylle, 1483. At the east end of the north aisle is a brass plate commemorating Sarah Anne Glover, 1891 who was the author of a form of Tonic Sol-Fa for teaching music.

St Margaret

Decorated west tower with traceried sound holes and two-light bell openings with flowing tracery. Diagonal buttresses rise to the bell opening stage and there is a battlemented parapet with large gargoyles. The four-light aisle windows are Perpendicular and have four centred arches. The south porch has spandrels enclosing figures of St Margaret and another amid foliage. Two bands of tracery are above and a stooled and canopied niche flanked by parvise windows. Within the porch is a tierceron vault and the south door has good tracery. Let into the wall of a brick vestry north of the chancel is a mediaeval crucifixion with figures, probably part of a churchyard calvary. It deserves better preservation. Within is a south aisle to both nave and chancel of two bays each, the piers octagonal with coved sides and rounded angles and four centred arches. Walls of the aisles are arcaded.

The font is on a high traceried step and the bowl has shields in quatrefoils. The eighteenth century reredos with the Commandments flanked with paintings of Moses and Aaron now hangs over the south doorway. Parts of the 1707 communion rails with dumb bell balusters now form part of the tower screen and gallery.

There is a fifteenth century chest and the Royal Arms of George I.

Monuments include a low tomb chest with a brass to Anne Rede, 1577, but the brass is a palimpsest of three, two English, 1370 and 1470 and a Flemish 1560.

St Martin at Oak

Named after an oak once growing in the churchyard in which, during the fifteenth century was exhibited an effigy of the Virgin called Our Lady of the Oak which became a source of revenue. Another oak was planted in 1656 and a further one in 1830. During the 1939-45 war the little church was bombed. It lay derelict until 1953 and now lives on as St Martin's Hall.

The tower has been stripped of its top stage, has a stepped parapet and has become a porch.

According to Blomefield the church was built before 1491 but like many another in the Saxon settlement of the ancient city it probably had a predecessor. The north side of the churchyard was lost to the church in 1882.

The north nave windows are Perpendicular with transoms. The south aisle arcade of four bays has slender piers of four shafts separated at the diagonals by a wave and a hollow chamfer. The aisle west window is a three-light under a square label flanked by two turrets, one leading to the tower the other to the south porch parvise. There is no clerestory and the nave roof sweeps down over the aisle.

The chancel, lower and narrower than the nave, was rebuilt in 1832, much care being taken to stick closely to the original plan. The windows have Decorated tracery set in deep wall arches. A small chapel, with Perpendicular windows extends south as an apparent extension of the aisle. Here is a monument to Jeremiah Rivans and wife in alabaster, 1727. Another commemorates a brewer, Thomas Newton who was Mayor of the city in 1722.

St Martin at Palace

This church stands in a unique position facing the great gateway to the Bishop's Palace. It replaces an older building that in turn probably replaced a Saxon building for it was on the borders of a probable Eastwyk settlement destroyed to make room for the great monastery. The church consists of a nave and chancel with clerestory aisles, a south porch with parvise and a square west tower. The last was restored and raised to its original height in 1874. Around the church Robert Kett and his followers fought and defeated the king's troops and slew their leader, Lord Sheffield, 1549.

A unique feature of the church are the three clerestory windows each side. They are square with enclosed quatrefoils in tracery. The tower is unbuttressed with two-light bell openings. The porch has two single lights over the entrance. The south doorway carries the rebus of Bishop Lyhart (1446-72) who is said to have completed the building. The porch is attached to the west bay of the south aisle which is of four bays with two large Perpendicular windows. It continues east to the chancel chapels. The north aisle is earlier. It too has an eastern extension to a chancel chapel.

Before the chancel hangs a lovely brass candelabra with an oval bowl inscribed as gift of John Wild, 1726. Behind the altar, hidden by curtains, are the Commandments (painted on metal plates.) The altar is a good Stuart table. In the Perpendicular east window are three figures on white surrounds signed as made in the William Morris factory.

Most interesting is the tomb chest of Lady Elizabeth Calthorpe, 1578. It is decorated with shields in strapwork fields separated by pilasters with a four centred back arch between them. In the spandrels are medallions and leaf sprays. Above are three arches, the two outer gabled, the middle semicircular, each containing achievements and their mantlings.

The font is octagonal with a panelled shaft and a bowl with shields in cusped panels, a moulded corona and a traceried bowl with battlement mould top and bottom. Seating is within panel-ended pews each with its door and the pulpit is in the same vein, looking late Georgian.

St Mary Coslany

A round towered church amid one of the largest churchyards in the city but low-lying and often in the past subject to flooding. The Saxon tower is all that is left of the original foundation. It has unquoined bifora with angled heads on plain imposts and a mid-wall cap supported by a banded baluster shaft. One must assume this as correct following a rebuilding in 1908. The rest of the church was built 1477.

The stone built ashlar porch is groined and has a parvise over with two windows flanking a stooled and canopied niche. On its west side is the parvise turret stairway. The church is cruciform with nave, chancel and transepts but no aisles, in fact a similar plan as that of St Peter Hungate and of Stody in the county. In the chancel is one Decorated north window and traces of a Decorated east window overlaid by the present Perpendicular. The rest is Perpendicular of c. 1470, the windows with two-centred arches.

The arch braced roofs of nave chancel and transepts produce a pleasing arrangement of diagonal ribs above the crossing. In the centre boss is the Virgin surrounded by rays and there are angels at the intersections of the purlins. The chancel roof is panelled with tracery, gilded on the bay over the altar. The chancel walls are arcaded, there are six plain misericords and the Communion rails are late seventeenth century with dumb bell balusters.

In the south transept is a piscina with a traceried head.

The parvise contains a fourteenth century iron bound chest and above the north porch was once a little nineteenth century schoolroom.

The font is octagonal with a panelled shaft and a bowl with shields in cusped fields. The tall font cover is seventeenth century.

The church has been associated with members of the Norwich School of painters, Daniell, John Sell Cotman, Crome and Robert Ladbroke.

On the east wall on either side the altar are faint traces of various texts in black letter. In 1547 a painter was paid five marks "for wryting upon the walls in the church necessary scriptures". These were painted before the Authorised Version of 1611. There are two sanctuary chairs with carved backs and the reading desk incorporates Jacobean carved panels. Two old bench ends with a massive seat between them still survive.

On the north chancel wall is a recessed monument reminiscent of an Easter Sepulchre, the tomb of a Dutchman, one Martin Van Kurnbeck, a Doctor of Medicine, 1578. Figures of the Doctor and his wife kneel facing each other, cut in stone. At the end of the inscription is a prayer for their souls, unusual at this date.

The pulpit is a composition of several periods. It began as a fifteenth century chalice pulpit, its linenfold panels being of this period. Later it was set on an octagonal base supported by eight turned balusters. An iron bracket holds the hourglass. It still shows traces of gilding for which the churchwardens paid 5/- in 1609. A new hourglass was bought in 1635.

The chest pre-dates the present church. It is completely iron bound and stands on six iron feet, has five locks and an iron bar passes through four staples.

At the west end, an unusual position, was the altar to the Holy Trinity. Could there have been, from Saxon times, tradition of an altar in that position? It was founded by Thomas Lincoln who twice served as city bailiff in 1275 and 1281. A tablet in the wall commemorates this in Norman French. "I Thomas de Lincole have given to this altar a torch and lamp and the rent in Colegate." Dated 1298.

St Michael at Coslany

By situation and dedication both St Mary and St Michael Coslany are some of the earliest foundations in the city. Coslany refers to an "island" in the Wensum's watermeadows where there grew up one of the isolated Saxon settlements that later fused together as a single community.

The church consists of a west tower, north porch, nave with north and south aisles and chancel. Mainly Perpendicular it replaces an earlier church which in turn must have been built on the foundations of a Saxo-Norman church.

Both tower and exterior are impressive and the flushwork at the east end of the Thorpe Chapel and the chancel (refaced in 1883) is the most sumptuous example in the country. The remarkable imitation window tracery worked out in white stone against the blue-grey of knapped and cut flint is attractive and is wedded to a parapet of flushwork in quatrefoils.

The west tower is more plain. It has flush panelled buttresses and a stone parapet with shields in lozenges and small pyramid crowned pinnacles. The bell openings are three-light mocked by three-lights at the ringing stage, blank on the east, south and north and glazed on the west. The Perpendicular west window is four-light flanked with stooled, canopied niches with finials. Below a frieze of shields is the handsome west door with tracery and figures illustrated by Cotman. The casement mould has shields in quatrefoils with tracery each side. A fine panelled base course connects tower and aisles.

Both aisles have large Perpendicular windows. There is a small north doorway below a shortened window and a blocked north chancel door. The Perpendicular windows have up and down transoms with tracery under the transoms.

Entrance is by an insignificant south door that could once have had a porch. It is set in a portion of the south wall that has been surfaced with ashlar. The nave is high and wide, brilliantly lighted by its great aisle windows all set in wall arches.

The four bay arcades (two on the south are missing) have piers of four shafts with a wave and long shallow hollow in the diagonals and the arches are four centred.

The fifteenth century font is octagonal, simple, with quatrefoils. The door to the sacristy has good tracery work. Some fragments of early glass are in the north aisle east window. Monuments include brasses with effigies in shrouds, one to Henry Scottowe, Alderman, 1515 and Alicia his wife, the other to Richard Ffrench, four times Mayor of Norwich, 1501. The north aisle and chapel of St John the Baptist were built by William Ramsey, twice Mayor, 1502 and 1508. The tomb chest in the chapel is his. The Thorpe Chapel, dedicated to the Virgin Mary was built by Robert Thorpe during the reign of Henry VII.

The organ is by Norman Bros, 1884. It was built for the Fisheries Exhibition, London, of that year.

St Michael at Plea

In this church the Archdeacon used to hold his "plea" or court. The building is Perpendicular, cruciform, consisting of a nave, chancel, transepts and north and south chancel chapels dedicated to the Virgin and St John.

This was the most important of the ring of churches that surrounded Tombland, the focal point or meeting place of the pre-Conquest Saxon settlement.

The west tower is stumpy, its pinnacles, a fanciful idea of the 1893 restoration, are ugly. The buttresses are diagonal, flush panelled with deep set-offs. The body of the church is flint but the porch, abutting onto the tower is ashlar faced, has a parvise lighted with two one-light windows flanking a stooled and richly canopied niche. Below is a frieze consisting of crowned Ms. The entrance arch is flanked with stooled niches, their finials crocketed. In the spandrels are figures of St Michael and the Dragon. The whole is contained between neat flanking buttresses. The south door is traceried with a band of quatrefoils surrounding it.

The arch braced roof has a brattished cornice and is curiously arch-braced between the wall posts. At the ridge are angels holding shields.

The fifteenth century font is octagonal, has a simple panelled and traceried bowl with a shaft similarly decorated but with quatrefoils as a sub-base. The seventeenth century cover is raised on four classical colonettes surmounted with a simple entablature and cornice, the whole under eight slim curved buttresses meeting beneath an open pinnacle on which stands a dove. The early fifteenth century screen paintings are now in the Cathedral.

The church is plentifully besprinkled with Aldermanic monuments of those who had been Mayors once and sometimes twice. Of these, brasses commemorate the Ferrers family 1530, 1577 and 1616. Jacques de Hem, 1603, has a black letter inscription with, to its right, incised kneeling figures and, over all, a pediment with macabre decoration of shovel, pick, skull and crossbones. Names of later Mayors are affixed to the eighteenth century wrought iron mace and sword rests.

St Peter, Hungate

This church, declared redundant some 40 years ago, is now employed as a museum of ecclesiology, the first church to be so used in the country. The present building replaces one ruinous in 1458 and was built by John and Margaret Paston, patrons of the benefice. Both Pastons and Berneys had city houses in the parish. The Pastons secured the patronage from the College of St Mary in the Fields in 1458.

Hungate is said to refer to Houndsgate where hunting hounds were kept for the Bishop's use.

The church consists of a truncated west tower with a flattish tiled pyramid on top, a nave, north and south transepts, chancel and south porch with a parvise and a north doorway. The steps down into the south porch probably indicate that the north doorway was the original entrance. On a buttress near the north doorway appears the date of the church's completion (1460) beside the carving of a dead tree trunk from the root of which is springing a new branch signifying the new church.

The parvise above the porch has a two-light window and is entered from the octagonal turret stairs on the west.

The nave is arcaded with four centred arches rising from piers in the walls that project 14″. In the east, piers are squints giving a view of the transept altars.

The large Perpendicular windows reach almost to the roof. The latter is a wonderful composition of low pitch with hammer beams and arch braces. At the crossing with the transepts are great cross ribs like vaulting allowing for the uniting of all four roofs with a great boss in the centre. The roof is similar in construction to those at Stody and St Mary Coslany, Norwich.

The fifteenth century font has a traceried bowl and shaft, the bowl having top and bottom battlement mould. The cover is seventeenth century. There is a stooled and canopied niche in the east wall of the south transept and beside it what seems to be a blocked squint. The floors are paved with Norfolk tiles.

The church contains some fine fifteenth century glass particularly that in the east window. The Royal Arms are those of George II.

St Peter, Mancroft

One of the most noble parish churches in England. While the interior contains much of interest and beauty it is the exterior that is paramount because of its unity of period and design. The whole church is Perpendicular completed in 1455 following a complete obliteration of the original church. Its position, in relation to the market place, the City Hall and the ancient guildhall, would have enhanced a less admirable edifice.

The tower is magnificent with rectangular buttresses niched, stooled and canopied in all stages and with a diminishing salient angle. The buttresses merge at the top with octagonal crocketed turrets. All is faced with stone panelling and between the stages on the north and west there are bands of quatrefoils. The west front has deeply recessed jambs to the doorway and two rows of ornament, one with shields in traceried panels and one with quatrefoils. Above this are ten stooled and traceried niches (a theme that is carried out on both north and south aisle buttresses). As a sub-base to these are twelve small deeply recessed panels with double cusps on the surface and shields at the back. A great west window bears the emblems of SS Peter and Paul in the spandrels. The tower is crowned with a beautiful flèche, probably a copy of that at East Harling (fifteenth century).

A double base course of flushwork and shields in rectangular tracery flows around the tower and north and south aisles. The south porch is vaulted but without a parvise, its entrance flanked with stooled and canopied niches. The north porch has lierne, cusped vaulting with a parvise above that once contained a library of books. The parvise has single light windows east and west. Holy water

Norwich St Peter Mancroft. Especial features the clerestory and the pinnacled niches.

stoops (modern) grace both sides of the porch entrance. The church is possessed of a processional walk beneath both tower and chancel, a piece of design occasioned by the enclosed nature of the site in the fifteenth century. The handsome clerestory has seventeen large three light windows, very narrow piers between them with little buttresses outside.

The interior is one of great elegance. Here is a lofty Perpendicular hall church with fine aisles and small transepts, the aisles extending into the chancel for all but the easternmost bays which are glazed to throw light on the altar. The lofty arcades have tall piers of quatrefoil section so undercut that they appear almost like detached shafts. There are canopied niches above the piers. The arch braced and hammerbeam roof has coving covering the hammerbeams. Long wall posts extend down to corbel heads, those on the south larger than those on the north. These in turn have niches below alternately reaching either to the arch summit or to the label stops. The roof is elaborately bossed with gilded stars over the nave, angels over the chancel.

The enlarged star above where originally stood the rood still carries a ring that supported the rowell light. There are angels at the ends of the hammer beams and a good cornice. The entire conception is similar to Ringland and Framlingham but on a larger scale.

At the east end of the sanctuary is a sacristy, long known as "The Treasury." It is a three storey structure, the top floor being the sacristy, below that a vestment chamber (it still has the beam from which the vestments hung) and beneath that a crypt. Here, in happier times was housed a rich collection of church plate, among it the famous Sir Peter Gleane cup and cover, given to the church in 1633 and probably the finest work of the period in existence.

The font is a seven sacrament one, fifteenth century. It has suffered much mutilation though there are still vestiges of colour remaining in the panels. The font canopy is magnificent, restoration having followed closely the original design — a close second to that at Trunch. Nearby is a thirteenth century hutch, probably the only relic of the earlier church. The handsome reredos is the work of Sir Ninian Comper, 1930, designed to mark the church's 500th birthday. The three mayoral sword and mace stands are work of the last three centuries.

A few stalls remain with simple misericords. It is interesting to note here that, during the nineteenth century restoration, large earthenware pots were found beneath the old stalls, undoubtedly intended to act as amplifiers. The organ case is contained in the south transept and is mainly eighteenth century work, with fluted columns and a pediment.

The east window has been described as a "bible of East Anglian fifteenth century glass". It contains 42 panels descriptive of Christ, the Virgin, St Peter, St John the Evangelist and St Francis, etc. All but seven panels are fifteenth century. It was possibly assembled in the window in 1741.

Of the many monuments the two to Sir Thomas Browne call for mention; both are south of the altar, the one put there by his wife when he was buried in the chancel, the other in 1922 when his skull was reverently re-buried after having been dug up and hawked around in 1840, finally to be put in a medical museum. There is a brass to Sir Peter Rede, 1568. Francis Windham, 1592, appears as a demi-figure on a large tomb chest with Tuscan columns and shields in strapwork.

The bells are famous, a peal of twelve and a tenor. In the sacristy is the "gotch" or ringers' jug, moulded by John Dearsley in 1749. It holds 17 quarts.

Most of the furnishing is Victorian and in perfect keeping with the church. R. M. Phipson who began drastic restoration in 1851 removed the Georgian box pews, the Laudian altar rails and pulpit. The tester of the pulpit is now a table top in the sacristy.

St Stephen

One of the great wool staple churches of the city, it replaced a former building known to have existed in 1285. Almost wholly rebuilt in the fourteenth century with later work done in the sixteenth century, it consists of a north-west tower embodying a porch, a hall-nave and chancel, north and south aisles and a small north transept or chapel. Absence of a chancel gives continuity to the eight bay arcade. In line with the north transept the north aisle roof carries painted panels, once the canopy of honour to an altar dedicated to St Thomas a Becket.

The general fabric is faced flint with flushwork on buttresses and tower. The latter, fourteenth century, has two friezes of flushwork emphasising the stages, the lower containing lozenges, the upper having diaper work surmounted with quatrefoils. In the top stage are bell openings flanked with blank two light flushwork windows. Above these on each side a circle, a lozenge and another circle in flushwork.

Above the west doorway is a frieze of small lozenges in the middle of which is the date 1550. The west window of 6 lights under its four centred arch is Perpendicular as is the east window of 5 lights under a two centred arch. The clerestory of 16 windows each side have narrow buttresses. West and east walls are ashlar faced.

The tower porch is vaulted and mid-fourteenth century. The bosses represent the stoning of Stephen and a scene at the death of Henry II when St Lawrence tries to rescue his soul from a demon. Other bosses depict emblems of the Evangelists and Apostles.

The interior gives a definite Tudor impression. The octagonal piers have sunk concave panels. Arches are in the main four centred and above is blank panelling. The hammer beam roof has traceried spandrels.

A considerable amount of old glass remains. In the east window it surrounds 5 large figures and groups of 1511 from the monastery of Mariawald in the Ruhr valley. Glass in the west window tracery is mid-nineteenth century and in a south aisle window the glass is by Kempe, 1905.

The church was once rich in brasses and a goodly number remain. Thomas Bokenham, 1460, Dr Thomas Cappe, vicar of St Stephen's, 1545, Richard Brasyer and his son (bell founders in Norwich and Richard was Mayor in 1510), also Robert Brasyer and wife (1510-15).

Many memorials decorate the walls. The earliest is to John Mingay and wife depicting them kneeling before a prie-dieu, 1617, the latest, a kneeling woman, to Lady Bignold, 1860. That to Charles and Mary Mackerell, 1727, is by John Ivory. Another to Elizabeth Coppin, 1812, interestingly combines classical with Gothic themes. Here too is the only monument in Norwich of Coade stone, an artificial product made by Coade and Seely of Lambeth.

A treasure of the church is an alabaster panel depicting nine saints, thought to have come from the reredos of the high altar of St Mary's College close by, dissolved at the Reformation.

St Peter, Parmentergate

The church of the mediaeval parmenters or parchment makers guild, set amid trees in a moderately large churchyard. The building is much as the rebuilders of 1486 left it. At the time considerable benefactions were showered on it. The east end is raised high and has a two storeyed vestry at its end (q. v. St Peter Mancroft) with a crypt below entered by a low south door.

The west tower has diagonal buttresses and a west doorway with two seated figures in the spandrels and a frieze of shields above it and traceried sound holes on north, south and west. The south porch, not vaulted, has a parvise with a two-light window and the south doorway has a hood mould with inturned head stops.

The wide nave has modern roofs and benches and lofty four-light Perpendicular windows, one on the north with a light obscured by the rood turret. There is a blocked north doorway below a shortened window.

The chancel arch is lofty with similar characteristics to the fenestration. Below is the lower part of a fifteenth century screen. Reputedly only the north half is genuine, the south part a copy. In its spandrels are well carved leaves, animals and figures, one being St Michael and a Dragon.

The four-light east window is nineteenth century, of sharp, bright colours. The fifteenth century font has four woodwoses (men of the woods) with clubs and shields standing between buttresses around the shaft and angels alternating with lions around the bowl.

Most ornate feature of the interior is in the chancel, the Berney monument of 1623. Looking rather like a four poster bed in coloured and black marble, it consists of a tomb chest by the south wall on which lie effigies of Richard and his wife, Elizabeth, in costumes of the period. The tester rests on four black marble columns. It in turn carries the Berney and Hobart quartered arms complete with supporters, crest and mantling.

St Saviour

In appearance possibly the most rural like of exteriors of all the city's churches. The tower is surely cut down, if the sound hole, now covered by a clock face is any indication. And one must conclude that the Decorated north and south bell openings were lowered and reset during one of the many restorations. The west window is interesting and the west doorway humble though the door tracery is good. The nave is wide, the nave roof sweeps low and the south gabled porch is an awkward projection though its entrance is moulded with decayed tracery in the spandrels. For a century the porch was used as a baptistery. The chancel is fourteenth century and its east window has reticulated tracery.

The west end is darkened by a gallery which looks late eighteenth century and rests on two cast iron pillars. It carries a neat little organ whose case seems to be of the same date as the gallery. Ungainly tie beams cross the nave below a plastered ceiling. Similar tie beams were removed from the chancel roof in 1923. Commandment Boards of metal still grace the east wall and below them is a good Stuart table.

The fourteenth century octagonal font is particularly good. The shaft is composed of clustered attached columns, separated by neat little pilasters and each column springs from the head of a beast. Each column has a traceried and canopied head. The bowl faces have quatrefoils in circles and the sides slope inwards.

There are two sword and mace rests carrying the names of twelve Mayors and there are a few good mural monuments.

SS Simon and Jude

Another of the city's churches whose fate has hung in the balance for more than a century. Once it stood within an ample churchyard but street widening has eroded it until today on three sides the church stands almost on the street. The west tower is unbuttressed and is half a ruin.

The nave is wide and aisleless. In the chancel is a doorway which has in one spandrel the figure of St Simon and in the other three fishes entwined (a Trinity symbol). The east window is unusual. It has widely spaced mullions incurving in the upper tracery to enclose large irregular foils. Encased in the chancel arch are the responds of a former tripartite form.

Within, the church has been stripped of furniture and fittings as it now serves as the Headquarters of the Norwich Scout Movement. This does not detract from its possessing features worthy of inspection.

These are the tombs of the Pettus family. That on the south is the earlier, to Thomas, Mayor of the city 1590. He lived close by in Pettus House. Dressed in his robes he faces his wife Christian, across a prayer desk with the family kneeling behind them, all in coloured alabaster. On the north the tomb of Sir John, Mayor 1608. In armour he rests on his elbow, the hand beneath the face holding a glove. Above his are two of his sons and four daughters and higher still, in a recessed arch kneels his son, Augustine, with his wife Abigail. For protection the tombs are encased in cupboarding.

St Swithin

One of the string of churches originally to have been built by the west highway running along the northern edge of the Wensum flood plain. The dedication is early Saxon. The present church, mainly Decorated, lost its tower in 1882 and the present pretty bell cote on the west gable of a roof that extends from west to east is Victorian. North and south clerestories are square headed two-lights and the north and south aisles have fenestration much as it was before restoration, that is, two-light Decorated with cusped tracery bearing above it a cusped quatrefoil. Both north windows are blocked. The rebuilt north turret led originally to the rood loft.

The four bay arcades were given strange restorative treatment, that on the south finishing up with square piers and semicircular arches, on the north retaining slightly hollowed out octagonal piers and four centred arches. The east window is five light with reticulated tracery. It contains two remnants of glass, one depicting the Trinity, the other symbols of the Sacrament.

The octagonal font was carefully restored. The eight faces carry symbols of the Trinity, the Sacrament, Instruments of the Passion and the three crowns of E. Anglia alternating with lions. The corona has angel heads and the shaft four stooled lions.

Some fragments of the old screen remain, one a panel depicting Edward the Confessor, found beneath one of the benches during restoration, and pieces of carved oak panels now incorporated in the reading desk.

A fine parish hall on the north side was made possible by a generous gift from an anonymous donor in 1908.

Among the monuments is one to the Suckling family dedicated to the memory of Lord Nelson's mother.

(For the last thirty years the church has been a furniture store. Happily the fabric and its contents have been carefully preserved.)

St Alban, Lakenham

A well designed modern church in brick and flint built 1932-38 by Cecil Upcher. The general design is traditional with polygonal east apse, a nave, aisles and west tower. The font is from Knettishall, Suffolk with tracery patterns on the bowl. An altar painting is by Jeffery Campe, 1955.

Furnishings of both nave and chancel is in light oak and the screen, erected as a War Memorial is in keeping.

St Catherine, Aylsham Road

1935 by A. D. R. Caröe and A. P. Robinson. The exterior is in pale purple and brown brick and is aesthetically good to look at in its small churchyard whose trees are now old enough to add their grace and shade.

The east tower has a saddleback roof. Under the west arch is the low projection of the baptistery. Inside are round concrete arches, side chapels with transverse arches all of which are connected by passages.

Christ Church, Church Avenue

1873 by J. H. Brown and Pearce. A church that combines early and mediaeval features, the former an apse the latter a nave with aisles. But the piers are stubby, with heavy bases and overloaded caps. and overmuch nailhead decoration in the arches. The windows are in the main plate tracery.

Christ Church, New Catton

1841-2 by John Brown. Of pale grey brick that has weathered to a dirty colour and with a great deal of stone dressing. All very much in E.E. style with lancets, sharply pointed arches and a wealth of engaged shafts, hood moulds, ball flower stops and pinnacles. The church has no aisles and the roof is open with queen posts and a ceiling above, all painted.

St Mark, Hall Road

By John Brown, 1844, the apse and vestry by J. H. Brown, 1864. The fabric is of flint and unpleasing yellow brick, the west tower is traditional but with polygonal buttresses and castellated turrets.

The wide nave has three galleries on iron shafts. Apart from these the church has a most attractive interior and a handsomely painted screen and rood loft extends across the church from north to south.

St Matthew, Rosary Road

Again by John Brown, 1851. Very heavy, dark and extremely neo-Norman. Built of ragstone which does not weather well in Norfolk air.

St Philip, Heigham Road

A later and more pleasing imitation of an E.E. exterior by Edward Power of London, 1871. It has a north-west tower with plate tracery bell openings and both nave and chancel have fenestration of a similar character. Recently made redundant.

St Thomas, Earlham Road

In red brick with stone dressings, lancet windows and no tower. It is by Ewan Christian, 1886. In layout it corresponds more to the hall churches of the West Country with aisles extending from west to east unbroken. There is no tower. The work is no longer Victorian, is restrained, creating an atmosphere of calm and spaciousness within. After war damage a very good ceiling was put in.

Presbyterian Church, Unthank Road

By B. M. Feilden, 1954-56, a building of steep gables and sharp angles everywhere. An effort to prove that the post-war world was different from the old in every aspect. Only the tower tries to be conventional.

Happily the exterior is weathering well and in consequence the general effect is not so startling. The church occupies an upper floor and subsidiary rooms, vestries and Sunday School rooms are below.

The church wears a bare, aseptic air and its ceiling is again broken into angles.

St John Baptist, St Giles' Gate. (R.C.)

A church frequently mistaken for a cathedral, often thought to be mediaeval, majestic, built on one of the highest points in Norwich, a monument to generosity and profound hope in the future of Roman Catholicism in Norfolk. It was built by the Duke of Norfolk, begun in 1884 and completed in 1910. It was designed by George Gilbert Scott Junior and, when he died in 1897 was continued by his brother, John Oldrid Scott. The style is E.E., the fenestration all lancets, flying buttresses for the clerestory, the overall shape cruciform. Inside, the nave is of nine bays with a triforium above, the chancel has four bays, the transepts three with eastern aisles. In addition there is a polygonal chapel to the north transept, a tall crossing tower and, in the south aisle of the nave, a chapel. All roofs are vaulted, quadripartite in the nave, ridge ribs with tierceron in the chancel. Porches and doorways are most sumptuous with recessed doors, much black marble pillaring and particular mention should be made of the west door to the north transept with its twin doorways and vivid carving in bas-relief above, reminiscent of Higham Ferrars, Northants. The baptistery lies west of the main north portal of the nave. Seating in the nave is of oak, low-backed, mediaeval style and uncomfortable. The organ has little to commend it.

Alphabetical List of Norfolk Churches

Acle,   St Edmund
Acre, South,   St George
Acre, West,   All Saints
Alburgh,   All Saints
Alby,   St Ethelbert
Aldborough,   St Mary
Aldeby,   St Mary
Alderford,   St John the Baptist
Anmer,   St Mary
Antingham,   St Margaret (St Mary in ruins)
Appleton,   (in ruins)
Arminghall,   St Mary
Ashby,   St Mary
Ashill,   St Nicholas
Ashmanhaugh,   St Swithin
Ashwellthorpe,   All Saints
Ashwicken,   All Saints
Aslacton,   St Michael
Attleborough,   St Mary
Attlebridge,   St Andrew
Aylmerton,   St John the Baptist
Aylsham,   St Michael
Babingley,   St Felix (ruinous)
Baconsthorpe,   St Mary
Bacton,   St Andrew
Bagthorpe,   St Mary
Bale,   All Saints
Banham,   St Mary
Banningham,   St Botolph
Barford,   St Botolph
Barmer,   All Saints
Barney,   St Mary
Barnham Broom,   SS Peter and Paul
Barningham,   St Mary
Barton Bendish,   St Andrew
Barton Turf,   St Michael
Bastwick,   (only tower remains)
Bawburgh,   SS Mary and Walstan
Bawdeswell,   All Saints
Bawsey,   St Michael (ruinous)
Bayfield,   St Margaret (ruinous)
Beckham,   St Helen and All Saints
Bedinham,   St Andrew
Beechamwell,   St Mary
Beeston Regis,   All Saints

Beeston,   St Lawrence
Beeston,   St Mary
Beetley,   St Mary Magdalene
Beighton,   All Saints
Belaugh,   St Peter
Bergh Apton,   SS Peter and Paul
Bessingham,   St Mary
Besthorpe,   All Saints
Bexwell,   St Mary
Bickerston,   St Andrew (ruinous)
Billingford (nr. Diss),   St Leonard
Billingford (nr. Dereham),   St Peter
Billockby,   All Saints
Binham,   St Mary
Bintree,   St Swithin
Bircham Newton,   St Mary
Bircham Tofts,   St Andrew (ruinous)
Bittering,   St Peter
Bixley,   St Wandregesilius
Blakeney,   St Nicholas
Blickling,   St Andrew
Blofield,   SS Andrew and Peter
Blo Norton,   St Andrew
Bodham,   All Saints
Bodney,   St Mary
Booton,   St Michael and All Saints
Boughton,   All Saints
Bowthorpe,   St Michael (ruinous)
Bracon Ash,   St Nicholas
Bradfield,   St Giles
Bramerton,   St Peter
Brampton,   St Peter
Brancaster,   St Mary
Brandiston,   St Nicholas
Brandon Parva,   All Saints
Braydeston,   St Michael
Breccles,   St Margaret
Bressingham,   St John the Baptist
Brettenham,   St Mary
Bridgham,   St Mary
Brinington,   St Maurice
Brinton,   St Andrew
Brisley,   St Bartholemew
Briston,   St Andrew
Brockdish,   SS Peter and Paul

Brooke, St Peter
Broome, St Michael
Brumstead, St Peter
Brundall, St Lawrence
Buckenham, St Nicholas
Buckenham Tofts, (no remains)
Bunwell, St Michael
Burgh next Aylsham, St Mary
Burgh, St Margaret
Burgh, St Peter
Burgh Parva, St Mary
Burlingham, St Andrew
Burlingham, St Edmund
Burlingham, St Peter
Burnham Deepdale, St Mary
Burnham Market, St Mary
Burnham Norton, St Margaret
Burnham Overy, St Clement
Burnham Sutton, St Ethelbert (ruins)
Burnham Thorpe, All Saints
Burnham Ulph, All Saints
Burston, St Mary
Buxton, St Andrew
Bylaugh, St Mary
Caister, Holy Trinity
Caistor, St Edmund
Caldecote, (few remains)
Calthorpe, St Margaret
Cantley, St Margaret
Carbroke, SS Peter and Paul
Carleton Forehoe, St Mary
Carleton Rode, All Saints
Carleton, St Peter
Castle Acre, St James
Castle Rising, St Lawrence
Caston, Holy Cross
Catfield, All Saints
Catton, St Margaret
Cawston, St Agnes
Chedgrave, All Saints
Claxton, St Andrew
Clenchwarton, St Margaret
Cley next the Sea, St Margaret
Clippesby, St Peter
Cockley Cley, All Saints
Cockthorpe, All Saints
Colby, St Giles
Colkirk, St Mary
Colney, St Andrew
Coltishall, St John the Baptist
Colton, St Andrew

Colveston, St Mary (fragments only)
Congham, St Andrew
Corpusty, St Peter
Costessey, St Edmund
Coston, St Michael
Cranwich, St Mary
Cranworth, St Mary
Crimplesham, St Mary
Cringleford, St Peter
Cromer, SS Peter and Paul
Crostwick, St Peter
Crostwight, All Saints
Crownthorpe, St James
Croxton (nr. Thetford), All Saints
Croxton (nr. Kettlestone), St John the Baptist
Denton, St Mary
Denver, St Mary
Deopham, St Andrew
Dersingham, St Nicholas
Dickleburgh, All Saints
Didlington, St Michael
Dilham, St Nicholas
Diss, St Mary
Ditchingham, St Mary
Docking, St Mary
Downham Market, St Edmund
Drayton, St Margaret
Dunston, St Remigius
Dunton, St Peter
Earlham, St Mary
Earsham, All Saints
East Barsham, All Saints
East Bilney, St Mary
East Bradenham, St Mary
East Dereham, St Nicholas
East Harling, SS Peter and Paul
East Lexham, St Andrew
East Ruston, St Mary
East Somerton, St Mary (ruins)
Easton, St Peter
East Raynham, St Mary
East Rudham, St Mary
East Tuddenham, All Saints
East Walton, St Mary
East Winch, All Saints
Eaton, St Andrew
Eccles (nr. Attleborough), St Mary
Eccles, (practically all gone)
Edgefield, SS Peter and Paul
Edingthorpe, All Saints
Egmere, (ruins)

Ellingham, St Mary
Elsing, St Mary
Emneth, St Edmund
Erpingham, St Mary
Fakenham, SS Peter and Paul
Felbrigg, St Margaret
Felmingham, St Andrew
Felthorpe, St Margaret
Feltwell, St Mary
Fersfield, St Andrew
Field Dalling, St Andrew
Filby, All Saints
Fincham, St Martin
Fishley, St Mary
Flitcham, St Mary
Flordon, St Michael and All Saints
Fordham, St Mary
Forncett, St Mary
Forncett, St Peter
Foulden, All Saints
Foulsham, Holy Innocents
Foxley, St Thomas
Framingham Earl, St Andrew
Framingham Pigot, St Andrew
Freethorpe, All Saints
Frenze, St Andrew
Frettenham, St Swithin
Fring, All Saints
Fritton, St Catherine
Fulmodeston, St Mary
Fundenhall, St Nicholas
Garboldisham, St John the Baptist
Garveston, St Mary
Gasthorpe, St Nicholas
Gateley, St Helen
Gayton, St Nicholas
Gayton Thorpe, St Mary
Gaywood, St Faith
Geldeston, St Michael
Gillingham, St Mary
Gimingham, All Saints
Gissing, St Mary
Glandford, St Martin
Godwick, (wholly decayed in 1602)
Gooderstone, St George
Gorleston, St Andrew
           St Peter the Apostle (R.C.)
           St Mary
Great Bircham, St Mary
Great Cressingham, St Michael
Great Dunham, St Andrew

Great Ellingham, St James
Great Fransham, All Saints
Great Massingham, St Mary
Great Melton, All Saints
Great Plumstead, St Mary
Great Ryburgh, St Andrew
Great Snoring, St Mary
Great Walsingham, St Peter
Great Yarmouth, St Nicholas
                 St Andrew
                 St George
                 St James
                 St John
                 St Mary (R.C.)
Gresham, All Saints
Gressinghall, St Mary
Grimston, St Botolph
Griston, SS Peter and Paul
Guestwick, St Peter
Guist, St Andrew
Gunthorpe, St Mary Gunton, St Andrew
Hackford, St Mary
Hackford, (see Reepham)
Haddiscoe, St Mary
Hainford, All Saints (the old church ruined)
Hales, St Margaret
Halvergate, SS Peter and Paul
Hanworth, St Bartholemew
Hapton, St Margaret
Happisburgh, St Mary
Hardingham, St George
Hardley, St Margaret
Hardwick, St Margaret
Hargham, All Saints
Harleston, St John the Baptist
Harpley, St Laurence
Hassingham, St Mary
Hautbois, Holy Trinity
Haveringland, St Peter
Heacham, St Mary
Heckingham, St Gregory
Hedenham, St Peter
Helhoughton, All Saints
Hellesdon, St Mary
Hellington, St John the Baptist
Hemblington, All Saints
Hempnall, St Margaret
Hempstead (nr. Lessingham), St Andrew
Hempstead (nr. Holt), All Saints
Hemsby, St Mary
Hempton, Holy Trinity

Hethel, All Saints
Hethersett, St Remigius
Hevingham, St Botolph
Heydon, SS Peter and Paul
Hickling, St Mary
Hilborough, All Saints
Hilgay, All Saints
Hillington, St Mary
Hindolveston, St George
Hindringham, St Martin
Hingham, St Andrew
Hockering, St Michael
Hockham, Holy Trinity
Hockwold, St Peter
Hoe, St Andrew
Holkham, St Withburga
Holme Hale, St Andrew
Holme next the Sea, St Mary
Holt, St Andrew
Honing, SS Peter and Paul
Honingham, St Andrew
Horning, St Benedict
Horningtoft, St Edmund
Horsey, All Saints
Horsford, All Saints
Horsham St. Faith, SS Mary and Andrew
Horstead, All Saints
Houghton St. Giles, St Giles
Houghton on the Hill, St Mary
Hoveton, St John
            St Peter
Howe, St Mary
Hunstanton, St Mary
                  St Edmund
Hunworth, St Laurence
Ickburgh, St Peter
Illington, St Andrew
Ingham, Holy Trinity
Ingoldsthorpe, St Michael
Ingworth, St Laurence
Intwood, All Saints
Irstead, St Michael
Itteringham, St Mary
Kelling, St Mary
Kempstone, St Paul
Kenninghall, St Mary
Keswick, All Saints
Ketteringham, St Peter
Kettlestone, All Saints
Kilverstone, St Andrew
Kimberley, St Peter

King's Lynn, St Margaret
                  St Nicholas
                  All Saints
                  St John the Evangelist
                  Our Lady of the Annunciation
Kirby Bedon, St Andrew
Kirby Cane, All Saints
Kirstead, St Margaret
Knapton, SS Peter and Paul
Lakenham, St John and All Saints
Lammas, St Andrew
Langford, St Andrew
Langham, SS Andrew and Mary
Langley, St Michael
Larling, St Ethelbert
Lessingham, Saints
Letheringsett, St Andrew
Letton, All Saints
Leiziate, All Saints
Limpenhoe, St Botolph
Lingwood, St Peter
Litcham, All Saints
Little Barningham, St Andrew
Little Cressingham, St Andrew
Little Dunham, St Margaret
Little Ellingham, St Peter
Little Fransham, St Mary
Little Massingham, St Andrew
Little Melton, St Mary and All Saints
Little Plumstead, SS Protase and Gervase
Little Ryburgh, All Saints (in ruins)
Little Snoring, St Andrew
Little Walsingham, St Mary
Little Witchingham, St Faith
Loddon, Holy Trinity
Longham, St Andrew
Long Stratton, St Mary
Ludham, St Catherine
Lynford, Church of Our Lady of
    Consolation
Lyng, St Margaret
Mannington, (in ruins)
Marham, Holy Trinity
Marlingford, St Mary
Marsham, All Saints
Martham, St Mary
Matlask, St Peter
Mattishall, All Saints
Mattishall Burgh, St Peter
Mautby, SS Peter and Paul
Melton Constable, St Peter

Merton, St Peter
Methwold, St George
Metton, St Andrew
Middleton, St Mary
Mileham, St John the Baptist
Morley, St Botolph
Morning Thorpe, St John the Baptist
Morston, All Saints
Morton on the Hill, St Margaret
Moulton St Mary, St Mary
Moulton St Michael, St Michael
Mulbarton, St Mary Magdalene
Mundford, St Leonard
Mundham, St Peter
Narborough, All Saints
Narford, St Mary
Neatishead, St Peter
Necton, All Saints
Needham, St Peter
New Buckenham, St Martin
New Catton, Christ Church
Newton, All Saints
Newton Flotman, St Mary
Nordelph, Holy Trinity
North Barningham, St Peter
North Barsham, All Saints
North Creake, St Mary
North Elmham, St Mary
North Lopham, St Nicholas
North Pickenham, St Andrew
Northrepps, St Mary
North Runcton, All Saints
North Tuddenham, St Mary
North Walsham, St Nicholas
Northwold, St Andrew
North Wootton, All Saints
Norton Subcourse, St Mary
Norwich, All Saints, All Saints Green
          St Andrew, Broad Street
          St Augustine, St Augustine Street
          St Benedict, St Benedict Street
            (tower only)
          St Clement, Colegate
          St Edmund, Fishergate
          St Etheldreda, King Street
          St George, Colegate
          St George, Tombland
          St Giles, St Giles Street
          St Helen, Bishopgate
          St James, Cowgate
          St John Baptist, Timberhill

St John de Sepulchre, Ber Street
St John Maddermarket,
   Maddermarket
St Julian, King Street
St Laurence, St Benedict Street
St Margaret, St Benedict Street
St Martin at Oak, Oak Street
St Martin at Palace, Palace Plain
St Mary at Coslany, St Mary Plain
St Mary the Less, Queen Street
St Michael at Coslany, Coslany
   Street
St Michael at Plea, Queen Street
St Peter Hungate, Princes Street
St Peter Mancroft, Market Place
St Peter Parmentergate, King Street
St Saviour, Magdalen Street
SS Simon and Jude, Wensum
   Street
St Stephen, Rampant Horse Street
St Swithin, St Benedict Street
Friends' Meeting House,
   Gildencroft
Friends' Meeting House, Upper
   Goat Lane
Octagon Chapel, Colegate
Old Meeting House, Colegate
Congregational Church, Princes
   Street
St Mary's Baptist Church, Duke
   Street
Outer Norwich, St Alban, Grove Walk
          St Catherine, Mile Cross
          Christ Church, Church Avenue
          Christ Church, New Catton
          Holy Trinity, Essex Street
          St Mark, Hall Road
          St Matthew, Rosary Road
          St Thomas, Earlham Road
          Presbyterian Church,
             Unthank Road
          St John the Baptist, St
             Giles Gate (R.C.)
          St George Fishergate,
             Sprowston Road (R.C.)
Old Buckenham, All Saints
Ormesby, St Mary
          St Michael
Oulton, SS Peter and Paul
Outwell, St Clement
Ovington, St John the Evangelist

Oxborough, St John the Evangelist
          Our Lady and St Margaret
          (R.C.)
Oxnead, St Michael
Oxwick, All Saints (ruined)
Paston, St Margaret
Pattesley, St John the Baptist
Pentney, St Mary Magdalene
Plumstead, St Michael
Poringland, All Saints
Postwick, All Saints
Potter Heigham, St Nicholas
Pulham Market, St Mary Magdalene
Pulham, St Mary
Quidenham, St Andrew
Rackheath, All Saints
Ranworth, St Helen
Raveningham, St Andrew
Redenhall, St Mary
Reeham, St John the Baptist
Reepham, St Michael
          St Mary
Repps, St Peter
Reymerston, St Peter
Riddlesworth, St Peter
Ridlington, St Peter
Ringland, St Peter
Ringstead, St Andrew
Rockland, All Saints
Rockland, St Mary
Rockland, St Peter
Rollesby, St George
Roudham, St Andrew
Rougham, St Mary
Roughton, St Mary
Roydon (nr. Diss), St Remigius
Roydon (nr. King's Lynn), All Saints
Runcton Holme, St James
Runhall, All Saints
Runham, SS Peter and Paul
Runton, Holy Trinity
Rushall, St Mary
Rushford, St John the Evangelist
Ryston, St Michael
Saham Toney, St George
Salhouse, All Saints
Salle, SS Peter and Paul
Salthouse, St Nicholas
Sandringham, St Mary Magdalene
Santon, All Saints
Saxlingham, St Margaret

Saxlingham Nethergate, St Mary
Saxthorpe, St Andrew
Scarning, SS Peter and Paul
Sco Ruston, St Michael
Scole, St Andrew
Scottow, All Saints
Scoulton, Holy Trinity
Sculthorpe, All Saints
Sea Palling, St Margaret
Sedgeford, St Mary
Seething, SS Mary and Remigius
Sharrington, All Saints
Shelfanger, All Saints
Shelton, St Mary
Shereford, St Nicholas
Sheringham. Upper, All Saints
Sheringham, St Peter
          St Joseph (R.C.)
Shernborne, SS Peter and Paul
Shimpling, St George
Shingham, St Botolph
Shipdham, All Saints
Shotesham, All Saints
          St Mary (ruins of St Martin)
Shouldham, All Saints
Shouldham Thorpe, St Mary
Shropham, St Peter
Sidestrand, St Michael
Sisland, St Mary
Skeyton, All Saints
Sloley, St Bartholemew
Smallburgh, St Peter
Snetterton, All Saints
Snettisham, St Mary
Southburgh, St Andrew
South Creake, St Mary
Southery, St Mary
South Lopham, St Andrew
South Pickenham, All Saints
South Raynham, St Martin
South Repps, St James of Compostella
South Runcton, St Andrew
South Walsham, St Mary
Southwood, St Edmund (in ruins)
South Wootton, St Mary
Sparham, St Mary
Spixworth, St Peter
Sporle, St Mary
Sprowston, SS Mary and Margaret
Stalham, St Mary
Stanfield, St Mary

Stanford,   All Saints
Stanhoe,   All Saints
Starston,   St Mary
Stibbard,   All Saints
Stiffkey,   St John the Baptist
Stockton,   St Michael
Stody,   St Mary
Stoke Ferry,   All Saints
Stoke Holy Cross,   Holy Trinity
Stokesby,   St Andrew
Stow Bardolph,   Holy Trinity
Stow Bedon,   St Botolph
Stradsett,   St Mary
Stratton,   St Michael
Stratton Strawless,   St Margaret
Strumpshaw,   St Peter
Suffield,   St Margaret
Surlingham,   St Mary
Sustead,   SS Peter and Paul
Sutton,   St Michael
Swaffham,   SS Peter and Paul
Swafield,   St Nicholas
Swainsthorpe,   St Peter
Swannington,   St Margaret
Swanton Abbot,   St Michael
Swanton Morley,   All Saints
Swanton Novers,   St Edmund
Swardeston,   St Mary
Syderstone,   St Mary
Tacolneston,   All Saints
Tasburgh,   St Mary
Tattersford,   St Margaret
Tattersett,   All Saints
Taverham,   St Edmund
Terrington St Clement,   St Clement
Terrington St John,   St John
Testerton,   St Remigius (in Ruins)
Tharston,   St Mary
Thelveton,   St Andrew
Thetford,   St Cuthbert
                St Mary the Less
                St Peter
Thompson,   St Martin
Thornage,   All Saints
Thornham,   All Saints
Thorpe Abbots,   All Saints
Thorpe next Haddiscoe,   St Matthias
Thorpe Market,   St Margaret
Threxton,   All Saints
Thrigby,   St Mary
Thurgarton,   All Saints

Thurlton,   All Saints
Thurne,   St Edmund
Thurning,   St Andrew
Thursford,   St Andrew
Thurton,   St Ethelbert
Thuxton,   St Paul
Thwaite,   All Saints
Thwaite St Mary,   St Mary
Tibenham,   All Saints
Tilney All Saints,   All Saints
Tilney cum Islington,   St Mary
Tilney St Lawrence,   St Lawrence
Titchwell,   St Mary
Tittleshall,   St Mary
Tivetshall,   St Margaret
Toft Monks,   St Margaret
Toftrees,   All Saints
Topcroft,   St Margaret
Tottenhill,   St Botolph
Tottington,   St Andrew
Trimingham,   St John the Baptist
Trowse Newton,   St Andrew
Trunch,   St Botolph
Tunstall,   SS Peter and Paul
Tunstead,   St Mary
Tuttington,   SS Peter and Paul
Twyford,   St Nicholas
Upton,   St Margaret
Upwell,   St Peter
Wacton,   All Saints
Walcott,   All Saints
Walpole S. Andrew,   St Andrew
Walpole St Peter,   St Peter
Walsoken,   All Saints
Warham All Saints,   All Saints
Warham St Mary,   St Mary
Waterden,   All Saints
Watlington,   SS Peter and Paul
Watton,   St Mary
Waxham,   St John
Weasenham All Saints,   All Saints
Weasenham St Peter,   St Peter
Weeting,   St Mary
Welborne,   All Saints
Wellingham,   St Andrew
Wells next the Sea,   St Nicholas
Welney,   St Mary
Wendling,   SS Peter and Paul
Wereham,   St Margaret
West Barsham,   Assumption
West Bilney,   St Cecilia

West Bradenham, St Andrew
West Dereham, St Andrew
Westfield, St Andrew
West Harling, All Saints
West Lexham, St Nicholas
West Lynn, St Peter
West Newton, SS Peter and Paul
Weston Longueville, All Saints
West Raynham, St Margaret (in ruins)
West Rudham, St Peter
West Somerton, St Mary
West Tofts, St Mary
West Walton, St Mary
Westwick, St Botolph
West Winch, St Mary
Weybourne, All Saints
Wheatacre, All Saints
Whinburgh, St Mary
Whissonsett, St Mary
Whitlingham, St Andrew (in ruins)
Wickhampton, St Andrew
Wicklewood, St Andrew and All Saints
Wickmere, St Andrew
Wiggenhall St Germans, St Germans
Wiggenhall St Mary, St Mary
Wiggenhall St Mary Magdalene, St Mary
 Magdalene
Wiggenhall St Peter, St Peter

Wighton, All Saints
Wilby, All Saints
Wilton, St James
Wimbotsham, St Mary
Winfarthing, St Mary
Winterton, Holy Trinity
Witton (nr. North Walsham), St Margaret
Witton (nr. Norwich), St Margaret
Wiveton, St Mary
Wolferton, St Peter
Woodbastwick, SS Fabian and Sebastian
Wood Dalling, St Andrew
Wood Norton, All Saints
Woodrising, St Nicholas
Woodton, All Saints
Wormegay, St Michael
Worstead, St Mary
Worthing, St Margaret
Wramplingham, SS Peter and Paul
Wreningham, All Saints
Wretham, St Ethelbert
Wretton, All Saints
Wroxham, St Mary
Wymondham, SS Mary and Thomas of
 Canterbury
Yaxham, St Peter
Yalverton, St Mary

Glossary

aedicule: miniature reproduction of a structural feature used for ornamental purposes.

apse: semicircular — or in some cases polygonal — end to a building.

arcade: a row of arches.

ashlar: freestone in thin slabs used as a facing.

baldachino: canopy borne on columns above an altar or throne.

baluster: miniature column of bulbous form.

banker: stone bench on which a mason dresses stone.

battlement: crenellated parapet.

bay: longitudinal division of a building.

bifora: two light window associated with Byzantine influence.

bolster: broad mason's chisel.

bond: method of arranging joints in walling so that no two appear immediately above each other.

brace: timber stiffener under tension.

brattice: a boarded partition.

bressumer: a beam extending across a wide opening.

buttress: masonry support of a wall against overturning pressure.

centering: temporary framework upon which an arch is turned.

chamfer: a bevilled edge.

clerestory: tier of small windows lighting the upper part of a building.

collar: short timber tying a pair of rafters together near the apex.

corbel: a stone bracket.

corbel table: a row of corbels carrying a tablement (q.v.).

core: inner part of a masonry wall.

couple: a pair of rafters joined at the apex.

course: layer of stones in masonry.

crocket: Gothic volute (q.v.) seen on sides of pinnacles, spires, gables.

crossing: space under a central tower.

cruciform: church having a central tower flanked with transepts.

cushion capital: Byzantine form of Doric capital seen in early Saxo-Norman work.

cusp: triangular tooth separating the foils (q.v.) in Gothic tracery.

dressings: dressed stone used in walling for lining openings and forming angles. Any worked stone as opposed to rubble.

drip-stone: projecting stone band over window to prevent water from wall over-running down glazing.

eaves: the roof projecting over the wall-face.

fan vault: late Gothic vault designed as a series of stone fans.

flushwork: East Anglian form of walling appearing as a pattern of stone tracery filled with knapped flint.

flying buttress: an arch carrying a thrust from a wall over to an isolated buttress.

foil: representation of a leaf. A small arc or space between the cusps of a window.

foliated: having a silhouette divided into a series of foils by cusps.

freestone: stone — properly speaking limestone — capable of being dressed by a mason.

frieze: middle or flat portion of an entablature (q.v.).

gargoyle: water spout draining a gutter, usually carved as a grotesque.

grisaille glass: thirteenth century work in greys and browns. Figure work severely straight, stiff, conventional of drapery.

groin: in early vaulting the line where two vaults meet.

hammer beam: end of a beam carried by a timber bracket from wall after middle of the beam has been cut away.

header: brick showing endways in a wall.

hood-mould: similar to a drip-stone (q.v.).

impost: springing line of arch, usually indicated by a moulded band.

jamb: side of a door opening.

king-post: central feature of a roof-truss (see truss).

lantern: central tower carried above surrounding roofs and there provided with windows for lighting the crossing below.

lierne: short decorative rib in Gothic vaulting.

lights: the divisions of a window.

lintel: horizontal beam bridging an opening.

masonry: dressed stonework laid in courses.

mensa: mediaeval stone altar table.

merlon: projecting portion of a battlemented parapet separating the embrasures.

moulding: running ornament formed of continuous lines of rolls and channels.

mullion: vertical stone member separating lights of a window.

ogee: a double curve.

order: a line of voussoirs (q.v.) in an arch carrying another over it.

parclose: a screen filling an arch (not the chancel arch) and enclosing a chapel.

parvise: "View of Paradise". The room above a porch.

paterae: ornament resembling a shallow dish.

pier: an isolated mass of masonry carrying an arch.

pilaster: a half pier projecting from a wall, usually employed decoratively.

pillar: a slender support.

piscina: stone basin set in the wall south of the altar for washing the sacred vessels.

pitch: angle of the roof with the horizontal.

purlin: horizontal roof timber passing between trusses (q.v.) to help support rafters.

putti: child figures either nude or in swaddling clothes.

quarry: diamond shaped piece of glass.

queen-posts: pairs of posts forming features of trusses.

quoin: angle strengthening the corner of a rubble walled building.

rafter: sloping roof timber carrying roof covering.

respond: end of an arcade or jamb of a single arch.

reticulated: window tracery organised like the meshes of a net.

ribs: slender members carrying a stone vault.

rood-beam: beam across the chancel arch to carry the Rood or Crucifix and associated figures.

rood-loft: gallery above the rood screen.

rood screen: traceried and pannelled screen usually of wood, painted and decorated, between nave and chancel.

rood-stair: stairs giving access to rood loft.

rubble: rough, undressed stone.

sanctuary: part of the chancel containing the altar.

scalloped capital: capital having its bell grooved in crude imitation of a Corinthian capital.

scoinson arch: carrying inner face of wall over opening.

sedilla: stone seats set in walling south of the altar.

shaft: diminutive of column.

spandrel: triangular space between arch and rectangular surround.

steeple: mediaeval word for a church tower. Renaissance spire.

stoup: basin for holy water outside the church door.

stretcher: brick lying lengthways in a wall.

string course: horizontal moulding used for linking features together.

strut: timber stiffener in compression.

tracery: system of bars in a Gothic window, seen also in flushwork wall decoration.

transept: lateral projection from a central tower, or from a central area usually one of a pair. Wider than a wing (q.v.).

transom: horizontal member of window tracery.

truss: system of timbering spanning a church and carrying purlins (q.v.).

tympanum: usually the wall space above the chancel arch. In mediaeval times covered by a painted Doom.

vault: stone ceiling.

volute: angle projection of Corinthian capital: in Gothic becomes a crocket.

voussoirs: wedge shaped stones that make up an arch.

wing: small projection from the eastern end of side wall of the nave.

Brief Guide to Periods and Dates relative to the Text

Saxon work: tenth century — 900-1050.

Saxo-Norman work: eleventh to twelfth century: about 1050-1200 period known as the overlap.

Early English (E.E.): Early Gothic: 1200-1300.

Decorated (Dec.): High Gothic. The phase of Gothic architecture in England roughly conforming to the fourteenth century. It is characterised by great use of decorative mouldings and more flowing window tracery than in the E.E. period.

The Black Death: terminated the Dec. period. At its worst during 1348-1352 it decimated the population.

Perpendicular (Perp.): Late Gothic. The last phase of Gothic architecture in England and dominating building during the fifteenth century and into the sixteenth as far as the Reformation, 1550.

The term "Gothic" is a generic term for architecture of England and the Continent over the period thirteen to the late sixteenth century.

Gothic Revival: Late eighteenth and nineteenth century.

Dissolution of the Monasteries: 1535-1538.

Reformation: Apart from the intermission of a return to Roman Catholicism during the reign of Mary Tudor 1553-1558 the Reformation lasted from 1538-1588. By the latter date the rise of a Puritan Nonconformity was becoming a power in the land.

The Puritan Commonwealth: 1649-1660.

Restoration of the Episcopacy: 1661.

Nonconformist Emancipation: 1689.

Catholic Emancipation: 1829.

Bibliography

THE DIM BEGINNINGS

The Christian Island   B. Saklatvala 1969.
Origins of the English People   B. Saklatvala 1969.
England Before the Norman Conquest   Oman
East Anglia   Rainbird Clarke 1960.
The Early Church in East Anglia   Margaret Gallyon 1973.
Historia Ecclesiastica Gentis Anglorum   Bede.
Beowulf   Trans. by Kevin Crossley-Holland 1973.
Sutton Hoo   Charles Green 1973.
The Sutton Hoo Ship Burial   R. Bruce-Mitford 1972.
The Times of St Dunstan   J. Armitage Robinson 1969.
The Anglo-Saxon — Studies in Some Aspects of their History   Edited by Peter Clemnor 1973.
Archaeology of Place Names   F. T. Wainwright 1962.

THE SAXON DIOCESE OF EAST ANGLIA

The Saxon Cathedral of North Elmham   A. W. Clapham and W. H. Godfrey (Antiquarian
    Journal 1916.)
A Thousand Years of Carstone   Claude J. W. Messent 1967.
Parish Churches of Norwich and Norfolk   Claude J. W. Messent 1936.
Excavations at North Elmham (Norfolk Archaeology Vol. 35 part III)   Peter Wade-Martin,
    B.A., Ph. D. 1972.
Anglo-Saxon England 1.   Edited by Peter Clemoes 1972.
Local Names in Norfolk   Munford 1870.
Penguin Dictionary of Saints   1965.
Aisleless Apsidal Churches of Great Britain.   Fairweather 1933.
Archaeology of Place Names   F. T. Wainwright 1962.
Domesday Studies: The Eastern Counties.   R. Welldon Finn 1967.

THE PRE-GOTHIC CHURCH AND BYZANTINE INFLUENCE

Introduction to Anglo-Saxon Architecture and Sculpture   E. A. Fisher 1969.
Anglo-Saxon Towers: An Architectural and Historical Study   E. A. Fisher 1969.
Architecture and Sculpture in Early Britain, Celtic, Saxon and Norman   R. F. Stoll 1972.
The Ancient Stones of Britain   Tudor Edwards.
Anglo-Saxon Architecture   Baldwin Brown 1928.
English Romanesque Architecture before the Conquest   A. W. Clapham 1930.

FOUR HUNDRED YEARS OF ARCHITECTURAL ADVENTURE

Parish Churches   Hugh Braun 1970.
Introduction to English Mediaeval Architecture   Hugh Braun 1968.
Suffolk and Norfolk   M. R. James 1930.
Suffolk Churches and their Treasures   Munro Cautley 1937.
Norfolk Churches   Munro Cautley 1949.
The Buildings of England Series   Pevsner 1962.

The King's England (Norfolk) Edited by Andrew Stephenson 1972.
The Pattern of English Building A. Clifton-Tayloe 1972.
The Norwich City Churches Claude J. W. Messent 1932.
The Old Churches of Norwich Spencer and Kent 1970.
Norfolk Churches Bryant.
Church Series. Norfolk (Two vols) Cox 1911.

THE GREAT DIVIDE: 1538 TO 1974

History of the English Speaking Peoples Churchill 1956.
Wren and his Place in European Architecture. Sekler 1956.
Six Hundred New Churches (1810-1856) M. H. Port 1961.
Nonconformist Church Architecture R. P. Jones 1914.
History of the Congregational Churches in Norfolk Browne.
Catholic Churches since 1623 Brian Little 1966.
Notes on Roman Catholicism in Norfolk Trapper-Lomax (typescript).
Catholic Faith in East Anglia Dom Henry Norbert-Biot O.S.B.
Dominicans in Norfolk Dr Augustus Jessop.
Before the Deluge Dr Augustus Jessop.
Costessey Stafford H. Jerningham.
Recusant Rolls — Lists of R. C. priests, late 16C and early 17C.
Norfolk County Churches and their Future The Norfolk Society 1972.
First and Last Loves (Nonconformist Architecture) John Betjeman 1969.

NORWICH CATHEDRAL: A GREAT BENEDICTINE PRIORY CHURCH

Guide to Norwich Cathedral John Britton 1817.
East Anglian Diocese: 1300th Anniversary. Editor, D. H. S. Cranage 1930.
Eastern Chapels of the Cathedral (Antiquarian Journal Vol. X11) D. H. S. Cranage 1932.
The Home of the Monk D. H. Cranage 1926.
Norwich Cathedral Priory Plan Arthur B. Whittingham 1948.
The Choir Stalls Arthur B. Whittingham 1948.
The Sculptured Bosses in the Roof of the Bauchon Chapel M. R. James 1908.
Sculptured Bosses in the Cloisters of Norwich Cathedral M. R. James 1911.
Norwich Cathedral Gilbert Thurlow 1972.

CHURCH IMAGERY

Penguin Dictionary of Saints 1965.
Drama and Imagery in English Mediaeval Churches M. D. Anderson 1963.
History and Imagery in British Churches M. D. Anderson 1971.
The Golden Bough James Fraser 1922.
The White Goddess Robert Graves 1948.
Dedication and Patron Saints of English Parish Churches Bond 1914.

FURNISHINGS OF THE CHURCH

Church Furnishings E. R. Delderfield 1966.
English Church Furniture Cox and Harvey 1908.
Baptismal Fonts Tyrrell Green 1928.
Ancient Coffers and Cupboards Cox 1902.

Index